CAMBRIDGE STUDIES
IN ENGLISH LEGAL HISTORY

Edited by
H. A. HOLLOND

*Fellow of Trinity College, Cambridge
and sometime Rouse Ball Professor of English Law;
Honorary Bencher of Lincoln's Inn*

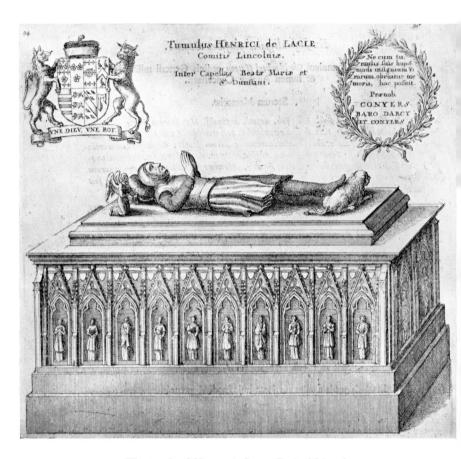

The tomb of Henry de Lacy, Earl of Lincoln

THE ORIGINS OF
LINCOLN'S INN

BY

SIR RONALD ROXBURGH

*Past Treasurer of the Honourable Society of
Lincoln's Inn*

Member of the Honourable Society of the Middle Temple

*Formerly one of Her Majesty's Judges of the High Court and
Whewell Scholar and Scholar of Trinity College in
the University of Cambridge*

CAMBRIDGE
AT THE UNIVERSITY PRESS
1963

PUBLISHED BY

THE SYNDICS OF THE CAMBRIDGE UNIVERSITY PRESS

Bentley House, 200 Euston Road, London, N.W.1
American Branch: 32 East 57th Street, New York 22, N.Y.
West African Office: P.O. Box 33, Ibadan, Nigeria

©

CAMBRIDGE UNIVERSITY PRESS

1963

Printed by The Broadwater Press Limited
Welwyn Garden City, Hertfordshire

CONTENTS

PLATES

GENERAL EDITOR'S PREFACE

IT gives me particular pleasure, as one of Sir Ronald's oldest Trinity friends, to welcome his fascinating contribution to this series. It may be regarded as a peace offering which he tenders, late in life, to the Muses whom he deserted for the forum. He makes with Sir William Ball and Sir Gerald Hurst a trio of Masters of the Bench, who have in the post-war period paid the tribute of authorship to their beloved Inn, which Hurst and Sir Ronald served in the annual office of Treasurer.

But whereas Ball's and Hurst's books were works of popularization, Sir Ronald's is one of exacting research and speculation. It will be found absorbing by those who pursue with it the teasing problem which it unfolds, and may stimulate some, as it has me, to attempt to visualize on the spot the rural surroundings in which early members of the Inn spent their working lives.

It has occurred to me that it may be helpful to those in whom this little book may stir an interest in the history of Lincoln's Inn if I append a list of works relevant to that subject which are in the Inn library. I am grateful for its compilation to the very learned librarian, Mr C. W. Ringrose.

H. A. H.

November 1962

LIST OF BOOKS AND ARTICLES IN LINCOLN'S INN LIBRARY CONTAINING MATTER RELEVANT TO THE HISTORY OF THE INN

ASHWORTH (M.). 'On Living in Lincoln's Inn'. *Cornhill Magazine*, No. 405 N.S. (1930).

BAILDON (W. P.). 'The Quincentenary of Lincoln's Inn, 1422–1922'. *Country Life* (1923).

BALL (SIR W.). *Lincoln's Inn; its History and Traditions* (1947).

BELLOT (H. H. L.). *Gray's Inn and Lincoln's Inn* (1925).

BRABROOK (SIR E. W.). 'The Honourable Society of Lincoln's Inn'. (Read in Lincoln's Inn Hall, 15 May 1873.) *Transactions of the London and Middlesex Archaeological Society*, Vol. IV (1875).

DUGDALE (W.). *Origines Juridiciales* (3rd ed., 1680). (Containing a Manuscript list of Armorial Bearings in the new buildings of Lincoln's Inn.)

HECKETHORN (C. W.). *Lincoln's Inn Fields and the localities adjacent; their Historical and Topographical Associations* (1896).

HERBERT (W.). *Antiquities of the Inns of Court and Chancery* (1804).

HUNTER (J.). Catalogue of the MSS. in the Lincoln's Inn Library (1838).

HURST (SIR G.). *A Short History of Lincoln's Inn* (1946).

HURST (SIR G.). *Lincoln's Inn Essays* (1949).

IRELAND (S.). *Picturesque Views, with an Historical account of the Inns of Court* (1800).

LANE (T.). *A Students' Guide through Lincoln's Inn*; containing an account of that Honourable Society, the forms of Admission, keeping Terms, etc. (1st ed., 1803; 2nd ed., 1805; 4th ed., 1823).

MELMOTH (W.). *The Great Importance of a Religious Life* (1849). (Containing Miscellaneous Notes. Persons buried under the Cloisters below Lincoln's Inn Chapel. Short notices of the Preachers of Lincoln's Inn. Sermons preached at the Warburton Lectures in Lincoln's Inn Chapel.)

PAYNE (J.). Lines written to commemorate the opening of Lincoln's Inn New Hall, 1845.

PEARCE (R. R.). *History of the Inns of Court* (1848).

POLLOCK (SIR F.). *The Origin of the Inns of Court* (1931). (An address given to Canadian guests at Lincoln's Inn, at a dinner on 21 July 1931. Also reprinted in Vol. 48 of *The Law Quarterly Review*, p. 163.)

RINGROSE (H.), *The Inns of Court; an historical description* (1919).

SELDEN SOCIETY (No. 71). *Readings and Moots at the Inns of Court in the 15th Century*; with an introduction by S. E. Thorne.

SIMPSON (SIR J. W.). *Some Account of the Old Hall of Lincoln's Inn* (1928).

SIMPSON (SIR J. W.). Inscriptions in the Undercroft of Lincoln's Inn Chapel. (Typescript) (1928).

SPILSBURY (W. H.). *Lincoln's Inn* (1850; 2nd ed., 1873).

THORPE (M. S. & C.). Lincoln's Inn Men, 1600–1919. (Typescript) 3 volumes (1921).

TURNER (G. J.). *Lincoln's Inn* (1903). (Pamphlet.): *The Origins of Lincoln's Inn* [from *The Athenaeum*, September 1906].

WAITE (W. F.). Clocks and Sundials of Lincoln's Inn. (Typescript) (1942).

WILLIAMS (E.). *Early Holborn and the Legal Quarter of London* (1927).

WOOD (L. J.). Drawings of the Hall and Library of Lincoln's Inn. (Portfolio) (1845).

WOOLER (T. J.). Case between Lincoln's Inn, the Court of King's Bench and Mr T. J. Wooler; with a critical commentary (1826).

Official documents of Lincoln's Inn

Catalogue of Printed Books in the Library of the Honourable Society (1859). Supplement (1890).

Εγκυκλοχορεία or Universal Motion, being part of that magnificent entertainment by the Noble Prince, de la Grange Lord Lieut., of Lincoln's Inn, presented to the High and Mighty Charles II. (Friday, 3 January 1662.)

Inscriptions on the Monuments or Gravestones under Lincoln's Inn Chapel, taken 9 June 1741, by William Sliford (Transcript of British Museum Lansdowne MS. 843).

Law Readings (MS.). [Maynard MS. No. 57.]

List of Arms in the Chapel made by Lord Hobhouse (MS.).

Record of the Celebrations, 28 November and 5 December 1922, commemorating the growth and prosperity of the Society during 500 years in one abode (1924).

Records of the Honourable Society of Lincoln's Inn (Black Books), edited in four volumes (1897–1902) by J. D. Walker and W. P. Baildon.

Transcript of a Middle Temple MS., on Lincoln's Inn, made by W. P. Baildon.

Treasurers of the Honourable Society of Lincoln's Inn, from 1586 onwards. Compiled by Sir Arthur Underhill (1925).

PREFACE

MANY sources of information have come to light since 1902, when Walker and Baildon completed their masterly edition of the Black Books of Lincoln's Inn. Outstanding among them is a seventeenth-century manuscript dealing with Lincoln's Inn and its associated Inns of Chancery which was presented to the Middle Temple in 1910. Baildon transcribed it in 1912. But nothing further was done, presumably owing to the outbreak of war in 1914, and the discovery passed almost unnoticed. I am grateful to the Masters of the Bench of the Middle Temple for allowing me to publish copious extracts from it, and also a plate illustrating two of its folios, and to the Benchers of Lincoln's Inn for permitting me to make free use of Baildon's transcript, and also of extensive extracts from the Black Books.

The publication of the more important parts of the Middle Temple manuscript must be pleaded as the main justification for this small volume. But some thirty years have gone by since Sir Frederick Pollock delivered to Canadian guests in the Hall an un-scripted address on the origins of Lincoln's Inn. All who heard it were thrilled with its brilliance, and it must always stand as a beacon for guidance in this ill-mapped field of legal research. But, although he did refer indirectly to G. J. Turner's important discovery in 1906 among the archives of the Abbey of Malmesbury of evidence of a Lincoln's Inn on a site in Holborn, the circumstances of the time and of the occasion precluded him from any consideration of the Middle Temple manuscript, or of the mass of relevant documents which had been unearthed by the industry of Elijah Williams, and published by him in 1927. This additional material is fully discussed in the following pages; and it is comforting to observe that an analysis of it appears to lead to conclusions not far removed from those of Sir Frederick Pollock, though at variance with those of many recent writers.

In these researches I have had unfailing help from Mr C. W. Ringrose, the Librarian of Lincoln's Inn, and Mr H. A. C. Sturgess, the Librarian of the Middle Temple, and from the staffs of both libraries, and I am eager to pay my debt of gratitude to them. I have pursued some inquiries at the Public Record Office, where Sir

David Evans, the Keeper of the Records (who has since retired), and Mr A. W. Mabbs kindly came to my aid, and also at the British Museum. There in the Manuscript Department Mr T. C. Skeat and Mr P. D. A. Harvey kindly studied the handwriting of the Middle Temple manuscript for me, and Mr S. J. Arthur was good enough to investigate obscurities in the rent roll in the chartulary of the Abbey of Malmesbury, and in the Department of Prints and Drawings Mr R. Williams kindly helped me to find the print of the tomb of the Earl of Lincoln which the Trustees of the Museum have allowed me to reproduce. There is a most significant reference to this tomb in the Middle Temple manuscript.

Finally, I am anxious to thank Professor H. A. Hollond. Without his encouragement this Discourse might not have been published; and throughout its preparation for the press he has guided me with much valued advice and most helpful suggestions.

R. F. R.

LAYHAM, SUFFOLK
November 1962

1

CHAPTER I

ANTIQUARIAN AND MODERN RESEARCH

STUDY of the origins and history of the Inns of Court became fashionable at the beginning of the seventeenth century. Fortescue in his treatise *De laudibus legum Angliae* (1468–71) had described them, but had given no account of their origin. The earliest written record has for long been assumed to be that contained in Stow's *Survey of London*, first published at the turn of the century (1598). Soon afterwards came Thynne's *Discourse of the Antiquity of the Houses of Law* which was almost certainly read before the Society of Antiquaries about 1600. This Society, which was the focal point of such studies, was founded about 1572,[1] and numbered amongst its founders Archbishop Parker, and William Camden, who was described as 'the most indefatigable antiquary and historian of his time' and was author of the 'incomparable *Britannia*'.[2] Included in its membership were Stow himself, Thynne, Cotton, William Hakewill (who at one time held the office of 'Register'),[3] Spelman, Lambard and Ley. Thynne, Hakewill,[4] Spelman and Ley were also members of Lincoln's Inn. The society, a '*Collegium Antiquariorum qui statis temporibus conveniunt et de rebus antiquariis conferunt*', met from time to time to hear papers upon selected subjects of antiquarian interest and discuss them.[5] It did so until 1604, but at about that time King James I suppressed it. It was not reconstituted until the eighteenth century.[6]

Thynne died in 1608, but his discourse survived in manuscript until 1720, when it was for the first time printed in Hearne's *Curious Discourses* in a group of four on the same subject.[7] This twentieth-century monograph appears to be the sort of 'curious discourse' which Thynne himself might have delivered if documents lately re-discovered had been at his disposal.

[1] *Archaeologia*, published by the reconstituted society in 1779, vol. I, p. iii.
[2] Hearne, 1771, vol. II, p. 425.   [3] *Archaeologia*, vol. I, p. x.
[4] In the four signatures which I have seen, he spelt his name 'Hakewil'.
[5] The first reference to the Society in print is to be found in Camden's *Britannia*. published in 1607. He wrote in reference to controversy about Brutus and Britain: '*Egone tantillus de re tanta cognoscere et statuere ausim? Rem integram ad Antiquitatis Senatum refero.*'   [6] *Archaeologia*, vol. I, p. xv.
[7] P. 108. A new and enlarged edition was printed in 1771. See vol. I, p. 70.

B

Close on his heels, and before Dugdale published his *Origines Juridiciales* in 1666, an author who cannot be positively identified, but may have been William Hakewill, compiled a manuscript, described later, which in its turn embodies extracts from a much older manuscript now lost. The lost manuscript was written by William Sulyard, probably about 1526 and certainly before 1540, and it contained the earliest account of the origins of Lincoln's Inn—and indeed the Inns of Court generally—which has so far come to light. The volume of seventeenth-century manuscripts which contains those extracts (and indeed much new or additional information on other subjects as well) is one of a series of three volumes which were presented to the Middle Temple in 1910 by the first Lord Reading and are now in the Library there. Of them he wrote later that 'it is believed that they were purchased from a descendant of the Blackstone Family' but that he had no further information with regard to them. The manuscripts, which are folio sheets written on both sides, were already separated into three volumes when they arrived in the Middle Temple, and they are now bound under three different titles. The first is described as 'Legal Antiquities: 17th century MS.' The volume relating mainly to the Middle Temple is entitled 'A History of the Middle Temple by Sir Robert Brerewood 1634/ 1638'. The third volume relates to Lincoln's Inn, Thavie's Inn and Furnival's Inn. None of them has a title-page. It is probable, however, that all three volumes were intended to form part of a single ambitious work, compiled on a preconcerted plan and probably under the supervision of a single editor. Apparently it was to be a history of English law in general, and in particular of the Inns of Court and of Chancery. Indeed, although the sections relating to the Inns of Chancery have at some date been divided between Lincoln's Inn and the Middle Temple, it seems reasonable to infer that there was originally a consecutively paged volume devoted to all the Inns of Chancery,[1] and that companion volumes on the Inner Temple and Gray's Inn were in contemplation. Only the Lincoln's Inn volume has so far been transcribed. A cursory glance at the other two may, however, be not out of place.

The first twenty-six folios of the first volume seem to be a history of London, concluding with St Paul's Cathedral, and making a reference to the Earl of Lincoln's tomb there. Folios 27 to 107, des-

---

[1] For example the opening folio of the account of Thavie's Inn is no. 79 in the *M.T.MS*. But it seems to have been at some time fo. 376 of another MS.

cribed as *Liber primus*, look like a general history of law. The remaining folios (108–67) constitute the 'second booke', and appear to record the history of the Inns of Court and Chancery, with special reference to serjeants-at-law. The volume assigned to Sir Robert Brerewood deals with the Middle Temple, Clifford's Inn, Clement's Inn and Lyon's Inn, and its general pattern follows closely the lines of the Lincoln's Inn Manuscript. The section devoted to the Middle Temple ends at folio 98 with the words *finis hic*. Sir Robert Brerewood (1588–1654) was Reader at the Middle Temple in 1638, became a judge in 1644 and retired into private life after the execution of Charles I.

The ninety-two folios of the Lincoln's Inn volume of the trilogy (from now onwards referred to as the *M.T.MS.*) are severely torn on their right side, and this accounts for all the gaps which will be found in the extracts taken from it. Almost all the folios are written on both sides (the letter 'd' denoting the back) and have been written by several hands. They were transcribed before the first Great War by W. P. Baildon, and his transcription—a most careful and scholarly piece of work—was bound up with an unsigned and undated preface by him and placed in the Lincoln's Inn Library. The extracts in this discourse represent (unless otherwise stated) a transliteration into modern English spelling of his transcript, after comparison with the original manuscript.

If there ever was a title-page to the *M.T.MS.* it is missing; the author's name nowhere appears, and there is no direct evidence of authorship. But there is circumstantial evidence, derivable mainly from the manuscript itself, which may be strong enough to justify provisional attribution of the composition to William Hakewill. But it must be provisional only, because although the indirect evidence is fairly strong, there are passages in the manuscript which might have been expected to be in the author's own hand, and none of them is in his, or indeed in any other known handwriting.

The Public Record Office kindly supplied me with photostatic copies of two of his signatures, and the Librarian of the Inn, Mr Ringrose, found another in the Black Books. They have marked and characteristic features, of which there is no trace in the manuscript. On the other hand, among the considerable number of his works still preserved in England, there is no known sentence in his own hand, and it seems to have been his practice to have all his compositions and documents copied by clerks. Having had invaluable assistance from Mr T. C. Skeat of the Manuscript Department of the British Museum who kindly studied the manuscript for me, I feel able to submit that probably none of the writing in the *M.T.MS.* is that of the author, whoever he may have been. In these circumstances provisional identification of the work with Hakewill seems to be justified by the available indirect evidence, especially as Hakewill played an important, though little-known, part in the history of Lincoln's Inn.

He is described in the *M.T.MS.* (in a passage of which he may have been the author) as 'William Haquevill vulgo Hakewill of Checkers in the county of Buckingham, Esquire, late Solicitor and in Commission for the Right Royal Lady Anne of Denmark, Queen of England, consort to our late Sovereign Lord of famous memory, King James'.[1] His arms which, as is mentioned in another folio,[2] were placed in the west window of the chapel (since destroyed by enemy action), were: 'Or, a bend between 6 trefoyles slypped purpure', and they are reproduced in Dugdale's *Origines Juridiciales*[3] and in Prince's *Worthies of Devon*.[4] Hakewill was born in 1574 in Exeter, and was educated at Exeter College, Oxford; but he went down without taking a degree. He was admitted to Lincoln's Inn in 1598 and called to the Bar in 1606. As early as 1609 he is mentioned in the Black Book as an 'old possessor of chambers'[5] and Prince[6] suggests that his chief residence for a great part of his life may have been in the Inn. As a barrister of only five years standing, he was appointed a collector of subscriptions for the new chapel.[7] As kinsman and an executor he attended the funeral of Sir Thomas Bodley in 1613, and shortly afterwards an M.A. degree was conferred on him. In 1618 he had become solicitor to Queen Anne of Denmark, and was called to the Bench of Lincoln's Inn. He was a Governor from 1619 to 1648.[8] In 1620 he was appointed a member of the committee to examine 'the evidences of the House touching a demand by the Lord Bishop of Chichester of a rent of £6. 13s. 4d. to be issuing out of Lincoln's Inn'.[9] This was at an early stage in the controversy which led to a suit between the Bishop and the Inn which was tried by the King himself 'sitting in a chair of state' on 23 November 1635. Hakewill was one of the Inn's representatives there, and he and two other Benchers reported the proceedings in one of the best-known passages in the Black Books, although unfortunately the report is

---

[1] Fo. 48.   [2] Fo. 74d.   [3] P. 241.   [4] P. 404.   [5] B.B. II. 128.
[6] *Op. cit.*   [7] B.B. II. 140.   [8] Dugdale, *op. cit.* p. 264.   [9] B.B. II. 219.

ANTIQUARIAN AND MODERN RESEARCH 5

written in a clerical hand.[1] In 1622 he became treasurer for the chapel,[2] and in 1624 he was appointed Reader[3] (having previously been Reader at Thavie's Inn).[4] His 'Reading' is still extant, but again is not written in his own hand. He was Keeper of the Black Book in 1634[5] and Treasurer in 1638.[6] He is last mentioned in the Black Books in 1650, having in the meantime become a Master of the Chancery in Ordinary.[7] At dates between about 1610 and 1640 he served in various Parliaments, as appears from the Preface to his discourse, *The manner how statutes are enacted in Parliament*, published by him in 1641.

Having about thirty years past, the free use and perusal of all the journals of the Commons House of Parliament . . . and being unwilling to lose the advantage of that opportunity, I read them all through, and whatsoever I conceived to tend to the rule of this House (wherein I was the better enabled to judge, in respect I had served in divers Parliaments or Sessions of Parliament before that time) I reduced under apt Parliamentary titles.

Appended to this discourse was a list of Speakers, and the last entry was the name of William Lenthal 'learned in the Lawes, one of the Benchers and Readers of Lincolns-Inne, at the Parliament which began Nov.3 1640'. This, and a monograph on *The Liberty of the Subject against the pretended power of Impositions* (1641), were the only writings of his which were published during his life. He died in 1655, in the eightieth year of his age. After his death an enlargement of his discourse on the manner of enacting statutes was published in 1659, under the title *Modus tenendi Parliamentum*. He is described as 'one of the Benchers of Lincoln's Inn, a grave and judicious Counsellor at Law, one who had sat in divers Parliaments, and having out of his great reading and long conversation with antiquity extracted those remarkable observations whereof this book is composed'. Prynne in 1668, in his *Aurum Reginae*,[8] referred to an unprinted manuscript on the same theme written by Hakewill in 1605 and presented by him to Queen Anne (of Denmark). Prynne described him as a 'person well versed in the Records of the Exchequer and other Antiquities, afterwards a Bencher and Reader of Lincolnes Inne, my very good friend and acquaintance'. Two

[1] B.B. II. 332.   [2] *Ibid.* 238.
[3] *Ibid.* 253: 'Being about that time much resorted to for his great abilities in his profession.' *Athenae Oxonienses*, published in 1691/2, revised edition, 1817. III. col. 231.
[4] *Ibid.* 227.   [5] *Ibid.* 314.   [6] *Ibid.* 349.   [7] *Ibid.* 389.   [8] P. 123.

of Hakewill's discourses were later published in Hearne's collection.[1]

Even a cursory reading of the *M.T.MS.* revealed the author as a member of the Inn with easy access to all its records. It also disclosed his marked interest in heraldry, and it was reasonable to suppose that he was a resident Bencher in touch with the antiquarians of his day. These considerations led to a search among the members of the Society of Antiquaries. Of the four members who were also members of Lincoln's Inn, Thynne and Ley were excluded by the context. Sir Henry Spelman (1564?–1641) (as Mr Ringrose has suggested to me) is a possible author. He was admitted to the Inn in 1585–6, he became a member of the Society in 1593 and he lived in London from 1612 to 1641. He had in mind a great work on 'the grounds of the law from original records'; but he determined to postpone his researches into this subject until he had compiled a glossary of law terms. Only one volume of the glossary was completed in his lifetime, and there is no evidence that he ever reverted to his project of a book on the grounds of law. He was at work until 1638, and this covers the period during which the *M.T.MS.* was put together.[2] But he is never mentioned in the Black Books, and Hakewill may be preferred as a candidate for authorship upon two grounds: (1) Spelman's relationship with Lincoln's Inn does not seem to have been close, (2) his relationship with Dugdale was so close that if he had been the author of the *M.T.MS.* Dugdale would almost certainly have known of it, and in particular would have made some reference to the Sulyard manuscript in his *Origines Juridiciales*.

On the other hand, every subsequent discovery has been found to be consistent with the theory of Hakewill's authorship, and none discordant.

(1) The author's own style, where clearly identifiable in the *M.T.MS.*, is generally diffuse and bombastic. But his exuberance almost boils over in his full references to the Chapel. This new building (which he records as being 'fully finished before this day anno 1637') he describes as 'the only laudable and most beautiful and most renowned model for ecclesiastical use, and the divine worship of Almighty God within this Academy, and it is very like the same

---

[1] *Op. cit.* They were: 'The Antiquity of the Law of this Island' and 'On the Antiquity of the Christian Religion'.

[2] See Hearne, *op. cit.* II. 439, and article in the *Dictionary of National Biography*.

to continue immatcheable to future posteryty even to th' end'.[1] And
yet the voice of the Treasurer who collected the subscriptions is
never far away. 'The edifice', he writes, 'hath in the performance
thereof been an insupportable charge to this Honourable Society'[1]
and in another place he records that 'the Lord Hobart Chief Justice
of the Common pleas gave freely xl[li] to the building of the east
window of the chapel',[2] and in an earlier passage (written before
1626) he states that it had cost £3,500 or thereabouts.[3] In the earlier
passage he describes the consecration of the Chapel on Ascension
Day 1623, and refers to the sermon preached by the Dean of St
Paul's, Dr John Donne, a former Preacher to the Society. Of this he
says: 'he delivered a right rare and learned sermon to the auditory
present, the further particular whereof I leave untouched for that
the same is to be soon upon every stationer's stall to be perused in
print, at the instance and entreaty of the Masters of the Bench and
the whole Society there.'[4] The sermon was published in 1626.

Now Hakewill was an original collector of funds as early as 1611
and he became Treasurer of the collections in 1622. As such and as a
Bencher, he would naturally be present at the consecration in 1623,
and four days afterwards he brought the Instrument of Consecration to a Council meeting, and delivered it to the Council which
ordered that it should always thereafter be safely kept locked up
among the title-deeds of the House[5] (where it still is). There can be
little doubt that he was among the chief advocates for the printing of
the Dean's sermon.

(2) There are certain puzzling features about the *M.T.MS.* It is
a collection of material, not arranged in orderly sequence, inter-
spersed with passages or notes composed by the author himself. He
was engaged upon the compilation over a long period beginning at
the latest in 1620 and ending at the earliest in 1638. The phrase 'this
edition' turns up in several places at widely differing dates; and yet
if the work was being prepared for the press, this preparation had
hardly begun.

This seems to have been characteristic of Hakewill's literary output. Though he acquired vast learning in a number of fields, he
appears to have been little better than a compiler with a diffuse and
disorderly mind. Only two short works achieved publication while
he lived; and there were compelling reasons to prevent the publication of this manuscript after his death in 1655. It could not have

[1] Fo. 6.　　[2] Fo. 71.　　[3] Fo. 66.　　[4] Fo. 66d.　　[5] B.B. II. 243.

been got ready for publication at speed, and as Mr Ringrose has suggested, Dugdale's *Origines Juridiciales*, which must have been long in preparation before its publication in 1666, may well have stood in the way.

(3) Some support for Hakewill's authorship may be obtained by considering the persons mentioned in the manuscript, and in particular Thynne, Ley and Digges.

Francis Thynne was thirty years older than Hakewill (having been born in 1544 or 1545) and he died in 1608, probably before the earliest entry in the *M.T.MS.* He was admitted to Lincoln's Inn in 1561, but he is not thought to have had much (if any) practice in the courts. He 'pursued with ardour the study of the history and antiquities of England'.[1] He fell on evil days and was imprisoned for debt. His literary output on historical, heraldic and antiquarian themes was, however, considerable (though it did not attain a high standard) and in 1591–2 he became a member of the Society of Antiquaries. In 1602 he was created Lancaster Herald.

The author of the *M.T.MS.* describes him as 'an ingenious searcher of antiquities'[2] and quotes from a discourse then unpublished which he may be presumed to have read before the Society.[3] It seems reasonable to assume that it was there rather than in the Inn that the author became acquainted with it.

James Ley was born in 1552. He was called to the Bench in 1600.[4] From 1604 to 1608 he was Chief Justice of the King's Bench in Ireland:[5] in 1608 he was appointed Attorney of the Court of Wards and Liveries.[6] In 1609 he and another were appointed to view the 'arms' of the House.[7] The editors of the Black Books were not sure whether this referred to weapons, or the coat of arms; but the *M.T.MS.* and Ley's 'table on Vellum' would have removed their doubts. In 1609–10 he was Treasurer;[8] and he contributed to the Chapel in 1618.[9] From 1621 to 1625 he was Chief Justice of the King's Bench:[10] in 1625 he was appointed Lord Treasurer.[11] He had by then taken up residence in the Inn.[12] In 1626 he was created Earl of Marlborough.[13] He died in the Inn on 14 March 1629, aged seventy-seven.[14] He was a member of the Society of Antiquaries. Of him the *M.T.MS.* relates: 'This worthy person at the time

---

[1] *Dictionary of National Biography.*   [2] Fo. 2d.
[3] It was first published in 1720 in Hearne's *Curious Discourses.*
[4] B.B. II. 61.   [5] *Ibid.* 85, 116.   [6] *Ibid.* 116.   [7] *Ibid.* 118.
[8] *Ibid.* 124.   [9] *Ibid.* 203, 215.   [10] *Ibid.* 220, 243.   [11] *Ibid.* 267.
[12] *Ibid.* 258.   [13] *Ibid.* 260.   [14] *Ibid.* 291.

of this edition 1627 is Earl of Marlborough in the county of Wilts, and Lord Treasurer of England by due desert from our Gracious Sovereign King Charles,'[1] and in a later passage that 'being desirous to lead a private contemplative life in his old age, he betook himself to his ancient chambers in Lincoln's Inn where he died on the 14th March aº quarto of his said Majesty'.[2] During his lifetime, he had prepared a table on vellum setting forth the arms of the Readers from 1465, and after his death a title-page seems to have been attached, perhaps by Hakewill himself, because there seems to be here more than a trace of personal friendship, and the title-page is dated 1630 whereas Ley died in 1629. They certainly had many common interests—Lincoln's Inn, the Society of Antiquaries, heraldry and the Chapel.

Of this table on vellum the *M.T.MS.* records:[3]

In the Library within this House is a fair large table with vellum wherein is set forth the arms of divers gentlemen now or lately fellow members of this Honourable College in metal and colour and therewithal is exactly composed the names of such learned persons as from aº 5 of Ed. IV (1465) until of late time have been Readers there in the two vacations (for learning) of the year all of which have been collected and formed by the industrious and liberal hand of the Right Hon. Sir James Ley Knight and Baronet, late Lord Chief Justice of the King's Bench, after Lord High Treasurer of England and lastly Earl of Marlborough and Privy Counsellor to King James of perpetual memory and of King Charles, a mirror of virtue, learning and antiquity. 1630.

Yet no trace of it remains in the Library, and in the *M.T.MS.* while the names and heraldry are set out in great detail, the shields are blank.

Richard Digges was called to the Bar in 1589.[4] He became a Bencher of Lincoln's Inn in 1608, eight years after Ley and ten years before Hakewill, and he was an important figure in the Inn until he became a serjeant in 1623. He was autumn Reader in 1608,[5] Treasurer in 1616[6] and Lent Reader in 1618/19.[7] In that year he was a member of a committee concerned with raising funds for the Chapel, for which he made a contribution and he subscribed towards the west window in 1624.[8] In the *M.T.MS.* he is correctly described as late one of the Benchers of Lincoln's Inn and now

[1] Fo. 71d. [2] Fo. 76d. He is there called 'Leigh'. [3] Fo. 8.
[4] B.B. II. 12. [5] *Ibid.* 114. [6] *Ibid.* 189. [7] *Ibid.* 208.
[8] *Ibid.* 201, 203, 450.

Serjeant-at-law.[1] It was from him that the author obtained a version of the rent roll of Thomas de Lincoln's Inn, which is discussed in Chapter IV. The recorded lives of Thynne, Ley and Digges, and their interests, are just those which would be expected in persons closely associated with Hakewill.

(4) There are many passages in the text of the manuscript of which Hakewill was well suited to be the author. For example, the *M.T.MS.* contains a summary of the relations between the Bishop of Chichester and the Society[2] described as 'well approved by the Archives of this House, memorably preserved and kept in the same' together with the text of certain deeds of title, including the conveyance of the freehold to William and Eustace Sulyard dated 1 July 1536. This part of the narrative concludes

after all the said estates performed, the Ancients or Benchers of this House, for good consideration acquired of Sir Edward Suliard, Knight, the said premises, who was the son and heir of the said Eustace Suliard the survivor... The Deed of Purchase from Edward is dated November Anno 22 Elizabethae, and seisin and possession was accordingly thereupon had and executed by the said Edward unto Richard Kingsmill Esquior to the use of the said Richard and other his co-feoffees and their heirs.

There is of course no new information in this summary; but it could well come from the pen of a man so closely associated with questions of the title of the Inn.

Again, the author's heraldic propensities, and also his diffuse and discursive style, are well illustrated by the long passage on heraldry inspired by a reference to the arms of the Society 'upon the frontispiece' of the great gatehouse. It extends from near the beginning of folio 7 almost to the end of folio 7d. But while this passage is in character with the writings of Hakewill, it must be admitted that it is also in character with much other writing of the period; and the evidence at present available does not seem strong enough to justify attaching Hakewill's name to the manuscript without reservation. Accordingly it must still remain the *M.T.MS.*

But although the search for the author has some fascination, his name is much less important than the contents of his work. The most valuable passages in it are those extracted by him from William Sulyard's manuscript which was then apparently in the archives of the Inn, though no trace of it can now be found there. It is intro-

[1] Fo. 5d.   [2] Fos. 3–5.

duced in the *M.T.MS.* in a passage which is unfortunately mutilated: 'In the ancient manuscripted books of this house... to have been written with the proper hand wrytinge . . . Sulyard Esquior who lived in anno 18 Hen.8'. This was the year 1526, and the passage may mean that the manuscript bore that date, which is quite possible, though it can only be said with certainty that it was written before 1540.

William Sulyard (who is first mentioned in the Black Books in 1514) played a notable part in the life of the Inn. He supervised much of the building in progress at that period, including a library, and in particular the great gatehouse in Chancery Lane, commonly associated since Stow's day with Sir Thomas Lovell, who made the largest donations to the cost. Sulyard was Pensioner in 1522, and records in his accounts that nobody came to demand the rent of Cottrell's Garden.[1] In 1523 he and another were assigned a Chamber in the Inn in consideration of the pain and labour he had taken about the building of the new gatehouse. He became a Bencher, Autumn Reader, Keeper of the Black Books and several times Auditor, and he was a Governor from 1531 to 1539. He took a new lease of the Inn premises from the Bishop of Chichester in 1535, and in the following year purchased the freehold (jointly with Eustace Sulyard) so that the Inn became their tenant. He died in 1540. The passages from his manuscript incorporated in the *M.T.MS.* are discussed in their appropriate places.

After Sulyard came Stow, whose account of the Inn is later considered in detail; and after Stow, Thynne. For his *Discourse*, although not printed until 1720, had been available to the author of the *M.T.MS.*[2] Indeed he made extensive use of it, as appears from the following excerpt:[3]

Also touching this House, called in Earl Lacy's days Lincolns Inn, it is mentioned part thereof to have been composed of the ruins of the Black Friars in Holborn, built of good stone, of whom and his mansion in Holborn thus chanteth a learned monk (Matthew Paris). And that the said Ralph Bishop of Chichester was Chancellor to K. H. III.

> Anno sub eodem [saith he] venerabilis Pater Episcopus Cicestrensis Radulphus de Nova-villa Cancellarius Angliae (vir) per omnia laudabilis et immota columna in regni negotiis fidelitatis Londini, in nobili Palatio suo quod a fundamentis non procul a Novo Templo construxerat, vitam temporalem terminavit.

[1] *Post*, p. 17.   [2] *Ante*, p. 1.   [3] Fo. 3.

This Bishop yielded to nature in Anno 29 H.III Anno domini 1244.

Of this Bishop and of the Black Friars, [my author (Thynne), an ingenious searcher of antiquities thus saith] Henry Lacy, Earl of Lincoln, Constable of Chester and guardian of England did erect a stately house which [saith he] according to the order of (most of the) other noblemen's houses, was after his title of honour called Lincoln's Inn wherein he made his chief abode and died about 4 or 5 K. Edw. I aᵒ salutis 1310 (sic). And this House [saith he] in the said Earl Lacy's days became an Inn of Court, greatly replenished with the sons of Noblemen and others generously inclined cohabiting therein together became students and professors of our common law.

The author of the *M.T.MS.* adopted these views, which were current at that time. Dugdale repeated them in his *Origines Juridiciales*, published in 1666,[1] but with a caution.

But in the next age [he wrote] Henry Lacy, Earl of Lincoln became possest thereof, and resided in it; whereupon, as many other great Houses did in those days make denomination from their owners, this had then accordingly the name of Lincolnes Inn, and hath ever since been so called. Of this Henry Earl of Lincolne, is the tradition still current amongst the Antients here; that he, about the beginning of King Edward the Seconds time, being a person well affected to the knowledge of the Laws, first brought in the professors of that honourable and necessary study, to settle in this place; but direct proof thereof from good Authority, I have not as yet seen any.

It is now possible to pass rapidly towards the close of the nineteenth century, because during the long intervening period of years no serious research into the origins of Lincoln's Inn was attempted, and no significant chance discoveries were made. But between the years 1897 and 1902 the late J. D. Walker and W. P. Baildon selected, annotated and expounded copious extracts from the records of the Society from 1422 to 1845, which were printed and published in four volumes (in this Discourse referred to as 'B.B.'). These records have long been known as the 'Black Book' or the 'Black Books'. The compiler of the *M.T.MS.* refers to 'the great Black Book of the house covered with black leather'; and 'the kepyng of the Black Boke'[2] has been the duty of an officer of the Society, now called 'the Keeper of the Black Books' and elected annually, from as early as 1511 until this day. The first of these books (no longer bound in black) is a small volume of some 180 folios, beginning in the first

---

[1] Ch. LXIV, p. 231.   [2] B.B. I. 163.

year of King Henry VI, and the whole series, still complete after the hazards of two world conflicts, is a treasure beyond price. 'Books of this type are not, of course, literature', wrote the late Sir Gerald Hurst in his *Short History of Lincoln's Inn*—'but for the historian or the antiquary, they are sheer delight.'[1]

The wealth and worth of research and exposition scattered throughout the four volumes of the printed extracts must win for Walker and Baildon the title of founders of modern research into the ancient history of the Inn. But since their work was done, there has been a notable accretion of new material, which seems to deserve systematic appraisal, and to compel reassessment of the problems.

When the *M.T.MS.* was rediscovered—by accident—Baildon set to work to transcribe it, and he completed his transcript and an introductory memorandum. But his task was interrupted by the outbreak of war in 1914, and he evidently made no close study of its implications before his death. Nothing further was done until Mr Ringrose brought the transcript to the notice of the author of this Discourse.

But this was by no means the only new material. G. J. Turner was engaged upon the history of the Inn as early as 1903, and at that time was advocating a theory that the Bishop of Chichester's Inn had previously been in the ownership of the Earl of Lincoln. But in 1906, by accident in the course of research, he discovered among the muniments of the Abbey of Malmesbury charters which revealed that in the fourteenth century there had been another inn called Lincoln's Inn in close proximity. This has been the most important discovery of this century in the field of this Discourse, and merits a separate chapter. Turner, who died in 1946, having indeed had ample time to reap the fruits of his discovery, had he been minded to do so, was fortunate in his biographer, since Sir Cecil Carr wrote a delightful sketch of his wayward, learned and inconclusive career.[2] He was a grandson of Lord Justice Turner, a collaborator with Maitland and a member of Lincoln's Inn. He worked for the Selden Society, his learning was vast and his research ubiquitous. Yet Maitland wrote of him in 1901 'his introduction to the Forest Pleas is a really good piece of work in the style of Madox. Unfortunately

[1] 1946, p. 1.
[2] *George James Turner, 1867–1946*, extracted from the *Proceedings of the British Academy*, vol. XL, p. 207.

he is the most dilatory of men and has tried the patience of the Selden Society to breaking point.'[1] This would seem to explain the disrupted and discursive character of his writings.

Turner died without carrying his investigations any further. But in the meantime Elijah Williams, F.R.G.S., who compiled two momentous volumes of documents and published them under the title *Early Holborn* in 1927, confirmed Turner's discovery, and proved conclusively that there was in the fourteenth century another Lincoln's Inn in the neighbourhood. He quoted or translated many ancient documents which he had discovered and which related to one or other of the three Lincoln's Inns which he found to have existed on different sites in close proximity—the Earl of Lincoln's Inn, Thomas de Lincoln's Inn and the Bishop of Chichester's Inn where the Honourable Society has been established since before 1422. Williams died in February 1937. He is still without a biographer, and efforts to include here a few words in tribute to his memory have failed through lack of sources of information.

But of his book, Sir William Holdsworth, reviewing it in *The Law Quarterly Review*,[2] wrote: 'Mr Williams has gathered together with great skill a mass of authority, which will smooth the paths of all local historians of this district, of all historians of English law, and, more especially, of all historians of the legal profession.' These documents will be referred to by the abbreviation W.D., followed by the appropriate number.

Among the muniments of the Abbey of Malmesbury discovered by Turner and translated by Williams was a rent roll of the property on which Thomas de Lincoln's Inn stood, as it was let in 1399. This document is of primary importance, because on its proper construction it shows that the premises then consisted, not merely of one Inn, but of two—one then newly built by the Abbot and the other, the Serjeant's Inn, in a state of decay; and it is fortunate that another and more complete version of this rent roll has come to light in the *M.T.MS.* This second version was, of course, unknown to both Turner and Williams. But long before he published his own book— in fact before 1913—Williams communicated in some way the contents of the other version to Dr Blake Odgers, because he in Essay No. 12 in the volume *Essays in Legal History* (edited by Vinogradoff),[3] after referring to the rent roll, added a note: 'for the above details as to the title of these various properties, I am indebted to

---

[1] P. 211.   [2] Vol. XLIV (1928), p. 386.   [3] (1913), pp. 250–5.

Mr E. Williams, who is in possession of the title deeds' and then proceeded to make extracts from it. The script in which that version of the rent roll is written is difficult to decipher, especially without the assistance of the version in the *M.T.MS.*; but Odgers' extracts are at variance with the text, and also with the translation which Williams afterwards published, and it was upon what seems to have been an erroneous reading of the document that he built up a theory which (in part at any rate) gained general acceptance. It will be submitted in due course that this acceptance ought to be revoked. Shortly stated, Odgers' theory was that there was on the property at that time only one Inn, that it had become ruinous, and that accordingly the Society moved out of it and into its present home between 1412 and 1422, taking the name with it. He rejected as legendary any connection with the Earl of Lincoln.

Holdsworth, in the second volume of the third edition of his *History of English Law*, apparently without independent investigation, accepted Odgers' theory as 'probably correct'. This theory will be discussed in detail in Chapter IV.

On 21 July 1931 Sir Frederick Pollock, Bart., as Treasurer, addressed the Canadian Guests of Lincoln's Inn upon the origins of the Inns of Court. That brilliant and unrehearsed address was shortly afterwards recorded in writing by Sir Frederick himself, and privately printed and circulated. It was also published in *The Law Quarterly Review*.[1] After prefacing his observations with the words 'If a categorical answer is demanded, the only safe one is that nobody knows', he accepted that part of Odgers' theory which predicated that the Society had once occupied Thomas de Lincoln's Inn.

It now appears [he said] that our predecessors did occupy a site in Holborn which in the fourteenth century belonged to one Thomas de Lincoln, King's Serjeant, and was described as *hospitium vocatum Lyncolnes Ynne*. That is a definite historical connection.

But he continued:

Must we therefore renounce Henry de Lacy and regard our appropriation of his lion as at best a trespass excusable by lapse of time? I suggest with diffidence that both tales may be true. Strange this may be, but often truth is very strange. Undistinguishable names of unrelated persons have before now occurred. . . Let the critical student think of the two

[1] Vol. XLVIII (1932), pp. 163–70.

William Penns of the Restoration time, and pause before he bids us take down our lion.

And of Henry de Lacy he said: the Earl of Lincoln

was an eminent and trusted minister of King Edward I. By tradition of which we have no written warrant we regard him as in some sort an eponymous patron of our early predecessors. His lion is borne on a canton in our coat of arms as finally approved by the Heralds' College in 1700. Earlier we had used the whole coat. It does not seem at all likely that such a tradition in a learned society had no foundation but a mere antiquary's guess.

Sir Gerald Hurst, in his *Short History of Lincoln's Inn*, adopted a similar line: he wrote in 1946:

About 1350 the Society occupied premises known as Lyncolnesynne from Thomas de Lincoln, King's Serjeant of Holborn, at a rent varying from £2 to £8 a year... Between 1412 and 1422 the Society migrated to a site on part of which the Old Hall now stands... The arms of Henry de Lacy, Earl of Lincoln... have long been borne as a canton on the coat of arms of the Inn in association with the 'mill-rinds' of the Kingsmill family. They were carved over the Gate House as early as 1518. Yet the Society's connection with the Earl is held by Holdsworth to be imaginary. He may, however, have been a patron.[1]

Sir William Ball, on the other hand, writing in 1947, declared: 'While there is some doubt as to the origin of the title "Lincoln's Inn", it was certainly not founded by any one of the name of Lincoln.' He then proceeds to reject the Earl as founder, but adds 'the Inn may have taken the name it bears from another man. In the fourteenth century it occupied a site in Holborn described as *Hospitium de Lyncolns Ynne* which belonged to one Thomas de Lincoln, King's Serjeant.'[2] There he left the problem.

The aim of this Discourse is to summarize and co-ordinate all the new material which has become available since Walker and Baildon finished their work, and to see whether it confirms or contradicts the ancient tradition or the modern theories.

[1] P. 5.   [2] *Lincoln's Inn*, pp. 1, 2.

CHAPTER II

THE BISHOP OF CHICHESTER'S INN

IT is certain that in 1422 the Honourable Society (a courtesy title of unknown origin) was already in possession of the larger part of its present site. It occupied the northern portion, which was known as Cottrell's garden, as tenant of the Hospital of Burton Lazars of Jerusalem in England. The Knights of St John had founded a hospital for lepers at Burton in Leicestershire, which was (in accordance with the prevailing custom) dedicated to St Lazarus of Jerusalem.[1] The Master of this Hospital was also Prior of St Giles' Hospital without London. William Cottrell was in possession of his garden in 1186. He made a gift of it to the Charity which created a rent-charge upon it of nine shillings a year, and this was the rent paid by the Inn.[2] The text of a receipt for payment has been preserved in the *M.T.MS.* It is in these words: 'Received by the Lord of St. John's by the handes of the Pentioner of Lincolnes Inne ix[s] quitt rent for Cottrell Garden.' To this the author of the *M.T.MS.* added the following note: 'This Cottrell Garden is the same plot of ground which is also called sometimes Conygarth, as the same is divided by brick walls.'

It occupied the southern portion of its premises, which included all the buildings which it took over, as tenant of the Bishops of Chichester, whose original title is still recalled by the adjacent 'Chichester Rents' and 'Bishop's Court'. The *M.T.MS.* gives a picturesque description of the site of the Inn, its boundaries and 'perambulations', which, though not expressly attributed to Sulyard, is almost certainly based on his earlier work. The description appears therefore to be in the main dated before the middle of the sixteenth century, and there had been no change of boundaries since 1422. It is as follows:

THE EXTENSION OF LINCOLN'S INN.
(being in three several parishes)

Lincoln's Inn, with the courts, curtilages, gardens, orchards and appurtenances thereto belonging, is situate in the parishes of St. Andrew in

---

[1] Williams, W.D. no. 1610.
[2] Williams, *Staple Inn* (1906), p. 51. See also W.D. nos. 1531, 1545.

C

Holborn, St. Dunstan in Fleet Street and St. Giles in the fields, viz. half the hall there, and all the buildings entirely northward with the new fair garden plot towards Holborn, in St. Andrew's parish: and the other half of the hall, with all the buildings southward is in the parish of St. Dunstan. And the fair gatehouse of brick is situate in both those parishes.[1] Also the Conygarth (*ab antiquo*) parcel of Cottrell garden, on the West part of the hall, is in the parish of St. Giles, as by a *meere* (boundary) stone signifying the same in the said Conygarth appeareth. Before the erecting of the said gatehouse of brick, there stood another gate at the north end of this House, which gate was kept fast shut all the whole year unless in the time of procession which was in ancient time held usually upon the Tuesday in *Gange* (Rogation) Week yearly. In which perambulation it was accustomed that the churchmen of St. Dunstan's parish did enter into this House at a gate at the South side thereof, and thence proceeded to the gate at the north end thereof towards Holborn, both which gates in those days were standing in mud walls, and that gate was it which is mentioned to have been kept shut all the year except in procession time and never opened but that one day yearly, being (as aforesaid) the Tuesday in Gange-week.

The soil of this House with(in) the parish of St. Dunstan beginneth at the South end side of the Conygarth, or Cottrell garden, and thence along into the hall much about the place where the now new erected screen[2] standeth, and thence the Churchmen with their procession issuing forth out of the hall go . . . n di . . . to the gate, and so into New Street or Chancery Lane, and against the middle part of the gatehouse they sang their gospel, whereby it appeareth that the gatehouse of brick is erected within both parishes. For before the gatehouse was erected St. Dunstan's procession, pacing along out of the hall . . . (the old gatehouse being then in the corner) did 'inviron' (go round) the well, now st . . . thence, out of the same gate into the street or lane aforesaid, and so . . . borne, till they came over against the houses where the now new erected gatehouse of brick standeth, and there the gospel was chanted.

Touching the like procession in those days made by the Churchmen of St. Andrew's parish in Gange-week, the same thus began. They came in at the gatehouse then in the corner, into the court, and thence passed along to the Chapel, where . . . was solemnly sung, and that ended, they issued into the hall . . . entertainment and decently sat down at the tables there . . . them provided, bread, beer and cheese, and that refection ended,

---

[1] This gate-house in Chancery Lane was built between 1518 and 1521 under the supervision of William Sulyard. Originally ornamented with a battlement, it was the main entrance to the Inn until the new hall was built in the nineteenth century.

[2] The screen, the work of Robert Lynton, and wrought on one side only, was placed in its present position in 1624.

they returned out of the hall and thence paced directly into Cottrell garden, or Conygarth, unto the door thereof, being then made of timber ... mud-wall at the north end of the Conygarth. And so pacing ... that door and certain houses there then built, issued thence in ... so away. And this is the manner of that perambulation.[1]

Moreover, there is no doubt about the Inn's title to its premises since 1422. The Society still possesses an unbroken record of its business since that date in its Black Books,[2] and although (as is natural) they have no historical preface, and there are some surprising omissions of important events, their evidence from that date until now is full, precise and accurate. The Society also still holds some of its muniments. But above all it has the remarkable distinction of a judgment in its favour, not merely by one of his Majesty's judges, but by King Charles I himself, sitting at Whitehall.

The Inn continued to hold its property as tenant of the Hospital of Burton Lazars and of the Bishops of Chichester until 1535. By a lease dated 6 December 1535 Bishop Sherborne demised 'all that greate house called Lincolne's Inne' to William Sulyard[3] for a term of ninety-nine years from Michaelmas 1535 at the yearly rent of ten marks. This lease, which was confirmed by the Dean and Chapter, is still preserved among the Society's deeds.[4] But very shortly afterwards, on 1 July 1536, his successor Bishop Sampson conveyed the house,[5] and purported to convey with it 'orto vocato le Conygarth, ab antiquo vocato Coterell Garden' to William and Eustace Sulyard to be holden by them and their heirs of the Lord Pryor of St John's of Jerusalem in England and his successors 'by fealtie only for all manner of services'.[6] By a deed dated 20 July 1536 the Bishop acknowledged the receipt of the purchase price of £200, and the deed of feoffment was confirmed by the Dean and Chapter on 1 August 1536.[7] A memorandum is written beneath the deed of 20 July 1536 to the effect that 'the houses and gardens on the south side of Lincoln's Inn be not comprised in my bargain, nor any part thereof, but remain to me and my successors, saving to Lincoln's Inn the setting of ladders and going in with stuff to repair the said House of Lincoln's Inn'.[8] William and Eustace Sulyard were brothers. William died without issue, and Edward, son of Eustace, by a deed dated

---

[1] Fos. 1d, 2. The edge of the MS. is torn, and this explains the gaps.
[2] *Ante*, p. 12.   [3] *Ante*, p. 11.   [4] B.B. II. 321; IV, 284.
[5] '*Totum illud messuagium nostrum vocatum Lyncolnes Inn.*'
[6] B.B. II. 321. The full latin text is set out in B.B. IV. 284.   [7] *Ibid.* 322.
[8] *Ibid.* 322.

12 November 1580 conveyed the premises in fee simple to Richard Kingsmill 'and all the rest of the Masters of the Bench of the House then and to their heirs'.[1] Between 1536 and 1580 the Inn paid rent to the Sulyard family.

Although William Sulyard recorded that as Pensioner in 1522 he did not pay the rent of nine shillings for Cotterell's garden because it was not demanded,[2] there is evidence of the payment of this rent to the Master of Burton Lazars as late as 1536,[3] and it is difficult to understand how the Bishop was in a position to convey the garden without the concurrence of the Hospital. But his purported conveyance seems to have been accepted and acted upon, because in 1546 the garden is described as '*late* parcel of the possessions of Burton Lazars'.[4] The point is of no practical importance because if the Society did not then get a good documentary title to it, it has long since acquired title by adverse possession, and no objection on this ground was taken in the dispute which broke out later between the Bishop and the Society.

This dispute seems to have begun in 1629, because on 11 June 1629 the Council appointed a committee, consisting of the Treasurer Edmond Estcourt, Hugh Cressy and Richard Taylor 'to search amongst the evidences of this House what conveyances they find were formerly made by any Bishop of Chichester to any of this House of any part thereof and of how much it was made'.[5] Estcourt and Cressy seem to have resigned from the committee, and William Powell appears to have taken their place, because at a Council held on 4 November 1634 a letter from the Bishop, Richard Mountague, was taken into consideration.[6] His complaint was threefold. First he claimed that the Inn had encroached about eighteen feet on the land of his see in Chancery Lane in the time of his predecessor Lancelot Andrews. He was Bishop from 1605 to 1609, and this complaint no doubt referred to the building at the south-east corner of the Inn which overlooked the yard of the Baptist's Head Tavern in Bishop's Court.[7] It was completed in 1609,[8] and is now numbered 24 Old Buildings. His second complaint was that the rent of £6. 13s. 4d. reserved by the lease of the house made by a Bishop of Chichester to William Sulyard in the thirty-fifth year of the reign of Henry VIII had been in arrear since he came to the see, and amounted to £40. He no doubt referred to the lease of 1535 reserving a rent

---

[1] B.B. II. 322.   [2] *Ante*, p. 11.   [3] B.B. I. 248.   [4] *Ibid.* 273.
[5] B.B. II. 285.   [6] *Ibid.* 320.   [7] *Ibid.* 177.   [8] *Ibid.* 127.

of ten marks, although that year was not the thirty-fifth of the reign of King Henry VIII. Thirdly he claimed that the inheritance of the whole site of the house was the inheritance of the Bishopric. This claim presumably extended to Cotterell's garden. Mr Powell and Mr Taylor, 'having been formerly committees in this cause' were entreated 'to review their former notes taken herein and if they see cause, once again to view the evidence[s] of the House' and to report.[1] This they did, and in their report, which was also signed by Henry Denn, after referring to the lease of 1535 and the conveyance of 1536, they observed:

So that it appears plainly the inheritance of the House was conveyed away as aforesaid, before any rent was due by the aforesaid lease, and it appears also that the said lease, if not extinguished, did end at St. Michael the Archangel last.[2]

Touching the encroachment they reported that:

two of us, viz. Henry Denn and Richard Taylor together with William Noye, now deceased, were present when Lancelot Andrews, then Bishop of Chichester, came to this House to view the laying of the foundation of the said building, and Sir Henry Hobart, then Attorney-General and one of the Masters of the Bench, then was present with the said Bishop, and they both together viewed the same, and had witnesses produced then, at which time the said Bishop received full satisfaction that this House by their foundation did not encroach upon any of his possessions adjoining, and so went away satisfied. And this view was made by the said Bishop in the year 1607 or near thereabouts.[2]

This report was presented to the Council on 20 November 1634. Shortly afterwards the Bishop sent a letter to the Recorder of London, Robert Mason, who was Treasurer, enclosing his case in support of his claim to the inheritance. The Council desired him to frame an answer, which he did. This was approved by the Council on 12 February 1635, and thereafter despatched. On receipt of it the Bishop appears to have sought the assistance of the Archbishop of Canterbury, because at a Council held on 21 April 1635 the Treasurer reported that he had received a letter from the Archbishop stating that 'His Majesty was pleased to hear the cause between this House and the Bishop of Chichester some time in the next Michaelmas term'. He was entreated to signify to His Grace that 'we shall be ready in all obedience to attend His Majesty at such time in Michael-

[1] *Ibid.* 320.   [2] *Ibid.* 322.

mas term as his Majesty shall be pleased to assign, we having convenient notice of the day and place'. The Council also requested
'such of the Benchers as have any way been employed in this cause
to meet in the meantime and prepare the cause for maintenance of
the title of this House against the Bishop of Chichester'.[1] At a
Council held on 13 October 1635 it was resolved to retain as counsel
for the Society Richard Lane, the Prince's Attorney, and Mr Cal-
thrope the Queen's Solicitor, and a committee was appointed 'to
prepare breviatts for instructinge of Counsell'.[2] On 17 November
1635, the Council, having received notice that the King had appointed the following Monday to hear the case, appointed the Recorder, Mr Hakewill,[3] Mr Taylor and Mr Glanvile, Masters of the
Bench, to attend.[4]

On 23 November 1635 King Charles I heard the case at Whitehall
'in the Withdrawinge Roome next the Bedchamber' in the presence
of William Laud, Archbishop of Canterbury, the Earl of Manches-
ter Lord Privy Seal, the Earl of Monmouth, Lord Cottington,
Chancellor of the Exchequer, Sir Thomas Edmonds, Treasurer of
the Household, Sir Thomas Jermyn, Vice-Chamberlain, and Sir
John Coke and Sir Francis Windebank, Secretaries of State.

The occasion was so rare, and the report to the Bench which
Hakewill, Taylor and Glanvile made on 28 January 1636 makes such
good reading, that it is here reproduced by the permission of the
Society from the printed edition of the Black Books,[5] with the original spelling.

The Bishopp, after he had kneeled down to his Matie sittinge in a
Chaire of State, and given thancks to his Matie for his grace and favour to
his Church in hearing of his cause upon his peticion, did enter into a discourse, wherein hee did intimate the over-increase of lawyers in these
tymes, vouching a transcript of King Edward the first to John de Metting-
ham, his Cheife Justice, that seaven-score lawyers were sufficient for this
whole kingdome; And also that the lawyers of Lincolne's Inne were not
incorporate, neither by Act of Parliament nor by any Letters Pattents
from the King's Matie; And made an appologie for his not havinge
Councell to plead his cause, inasmuch as he himselfe had spent some
time in reading of the bookes of the lawe, and would nowe invade upon
their profession, as some of them had done upon his.

(1) First, he did insist upon an incrochement, in the late buildinges of the
south parte of Lincolne's Inne, to the quantitie of fortie foote, upon his

[1] B.B. II. 324–5.   [2] Ibid. 329.   [3] Ante, p. 4.   [4] B.B. II. 331.
[5] Ibid. 332.

possessions, and did severall times vouche Mr Glanvile to justifie that the same had bene acknowledged by some of the lawyers of Lincolne's Inne.

Mr Glanvile, hearing himselfe soe often named, presented himselfe to his Matie, offering to speake upon oath, if his Matie pleased. And it being answered him that the Kinge would beleeve him without an oath, and his Matie sayinge 'Speak, Mr Glanvile,' hee did in expresse termes denye what my Lord Bishopp affirmed therein. And then Mr Recorder,[1] nowe deceased, shewed that Lancelott, late Lord B^PP,[2] came in person when the foundacion of those buildings (wherein the incrochement was supposed) were in layinge, and Sir Henry Hobart, then Attorney Generall to his Matie's father, did meete him, and ancient old men were examined in their presence, and hee was satisfied noe wronge was done, and offerred the testimonye herein of Sir Frauncis Kynaston, his Matie's servant, and of Mr Taylor, then present.

His Matie thought not fitt to insist upon an incrochement, the Petition conteyninge a title to the whole, using these words, 'That was a poore thinge and upon the Bye',[3] directinge the Bishopp to goe on to the matter.

(2) Secondlie, the Bishopp did shewe that hee did paie First Fruits to his Matie proporcionablye as he did for other of his possessions, and made a narrative of his tytle:—That Raphe de Nova villa, his predicessor, sometymes Chancellor of England, did obteyne from King Henrye the Third parte of that which is nowe Lincolne's Inne, and three gardens, neere a streete then called 'New Streete', after 'Chanceler Lane', and nowe 'Chancery Lane', whereof one of them was of the same side the Rolls is, the other two of the west side of the Lane; that the said Raphe de Nova villa, his predicessor, did build his Howse there, and there he lived and there he died; and that he settled or left those possessions to his Sea successive, as he did certeine howses neere Newgate to the Deane and Chapter of Chichester; and that which is nowe called 'Lincolne's Inne' was called 'Chichester Howse', and that some of his predicessors did lye there; and divers of his predicessors had made leases to the Benchers of Lincolne's Inne, and reserved rent, and lodgings in the Howse when they should repayre to London aboute their owne busines or his Matie's affaires; and that in the time of Henry the Seaventh, a lease was made by his predicessor unto Frauncis Syliard, a Bencher of Lincolne's Inne, and father of William Syliard, which continewed untill the time of the lease made by Robert Sherborne, one of his predicessors, to the said William Syliard in vicesimo septimo Henrici Octavi, for nynetie and nine yeres, under the yerelie rent of six pounds, thirteene shillings and fower pence, the which lease did end att Michaelmas, one thowsand, six hundred, thirtie and fower.

---

[1] Robert Mason.   [2] Lancelot Andrews.   [3] I.e. of little importance.

His Matie was pleased to saie that hee had told a smooth tale, and willed Mr Recorder not to insist upon what hee had prepared, but to acknowledge what was right and to contradict what was not.

Mr Recorder did not denye, but acknowledge, the tytle of the Bishopp's predicessors to the Howse, and insisted upon the lease of Robert Sherborne, his predicessor, to William Syliard for nynetie nyne yeres, and of the Deede of Graunt of the inheritance thereof unto the said William Syliard and Eustace, his brother, and to their heires, bearing date, primo die Julij, and confirmed by the Deane and Chapter under their seale primo Augusti followinge, both of them being produced under seale; and alsoe insisted upon the longe continewed possession.

His ma^tie was pleased to saie that if there were not a right, then the antiquitie of the possession was the longer continewance of a wronge.

(1) First the Bishopp in his reply did acknowledge that he did not till then thinck the Deane and Chapter had confirmed the Deede of Graunt of the inheritance made by Richard Sampson, his predicessor.

(2) Secondlye, hee made a discourse that his predicessor with the consent of his Deane and Chapter could not alien before the Statute in prejudice of succession, and insisted upon the aucthoritie of my Lord Cooke in his "Institutes", and in the Bishopp of Winchester's cause, and upon Bracton, affirminge his estate in trust, and they could not be barred who were not *in rerum natura.*

(3) And made mencion of the strange qualitie and nature, as he termed it, of Richard Sampson, (his predicessor that made the graunte), that he was in his beginning the Chaplyn to Robert Sherborne, his predicessor, and by this meanes was raised to be Deane of the Chappell to King Henrye the Eighth, and to be Deane of Windsor. And when Robert Sherborne, his old M^r, was nynetie two yeres old, he procured King Henry the Eighth to write his letters to him to resigne his Bishopwrick, and to content himselfe with fower hundred poundes per annum, and so procured to himselfe the Bishopwricke; and then made what hast he could to make awaie the possessions thereof to William Syliard and to Eustace, his brother, then one of the Ushers of King Henry the 8th Bedchamber, and, as is likelye, in some requitall for being a meanes to helpe him to his Bishoppwricke.

Mr Recorder begann his answeare with a wishe that my Lord Bishopp had had Councell, for they would not have insisted upon the premisses. And beginninge to declare what ye comon lawe was touching a Bishopp's alienacion with the consent of the Deane and Chapter, his Matie interrupted him, and directinge himselfe to the Bishopp said, 'If the lawe had bene as you saie, what then needed my father's statute[1] whereby they are respayned'? but did blame the Bishopp that did make the alienacion.

---

[1] 1 James I, c. 3. An Act against the diminution of the possessions of archbishopricks and bishopricks.

The Bishopp did not move or insist upon the pointe of the inabilitie of his predicessor to make the deede of the graunt of inheritance dated primo Julij, his restitucion of temporalities being quarto Julii, before he was putt in mynde thereof by my Lord Privie Seale. His Matie using these words—'This is the strongest argument I see yett, my Lord; I am afraide all your other will disceive yow if this hold not.'

To which Mr Recorder aunsweared that it should be presumed to be delivered after the fowrth of Julij, and the rather because it is usuall to putt in the dates of deeds when they are written and ingrossed; and it is a comon course to ante-date deedes, and not to post-date them; and the two hundred pounds which was to be paied, being a valuable consideracion for a revercion upon soe longe a lease, was not paied untill the twentith of Julij, as appeares by the indenture betweene the Bishopp and William and Eustace Syliard; and by reason of the longe continewed possession it should be soe presumed. And shewed how long continued possession was not onlie favoured by our Lawe, but by the Civill and Cannon Lawe, and that with them there was *tempus antiquum* (as thirtie yeres) where *extrinseca* should be presumed, and *tempus antiquissimum* (as one hundred yeres) where *intrinseca* should be presumed.

His Matie seeminge att the first not to be fullye satisfied with this answeare, Mr Recorder did further aunsweare that Richard Sampson, whoe made the Deede of Graunt of the inheritance, was elected Bishopp, and had the Royall assent, and was consecrated undecimo Junij before primo Julij when the deede beares date. And the inheritance of the lands of the Bishopwrick were vested in him before the restitucion of the temporalities. And albeit the Bishopp could not make a feoffment to execute livery before restitucion, because of the King's possession, yett here it did passe by waie of graunt of revercion and attornement, beinge made to William Syliard, the lessee, and to his brother Eustace, and their heires.

His Matie thereupon delivered his opinion that the conveyance was good, because, when he had the Royall assent and was consecrate, hee was full parson.

The Lord Privie Seale, having our Deede of Graunt of inheritance in his hands, after perusall thereof, did object (in the behalf of the Bishopp) that in the same there was a Letter of Attorney to deliver seisen, and therefore the intention was to passe by feoffement.

His ma^tie readilie made answeare ther unto *Abundantia bonorum non nocet*.

My Lord's Grace of Canterburye declared himselfe that the deede might well be delivered after the date.

His Matie, being fullie satisfied in ye former points insisted upon, directinge himselfe to Mr Recorder, saied, 'But what saie yow to the payment of First Fruits, and his beinge assessed in my bookes?'

To which Mr Recorder answeared that the First Fruits being settled by Commissions, and retorned into th' Eschequer, are not altered or apporcioned, unlesse it be in case when the alienacion is made to the Crowne, but not when it is made to a subject; and that that was the constant course of the Eschequer.

Wherewith his Matie was satisfied, and rose out of his chaire.

Nevertheles, my Lord Bishopp informed his Matie of two titles that his Matie had to Lincolne's Inne.

The first that the Frier Preachers had first a howse in New Streete given them by Hugh de Birch,[1] beinge that which the lawyers of Lincolne's Inne nowe hold;[2] and they beinge translated thence[3] by Robert Kilwarbe, the Archbishopp,[4] to a place near Baynard's Castle, nowe called Blackfriers, their house came to Henry Lacye, Earle of Lincolne; whose sonne beinge drowned in a well att Denbie Castle, Alice, his daughter, one of the greatest heires and greatest wantons of the kingdome, was married to Thomas Plantaginet, Earle of Lancaster. Allbeit shee had fower husbands, yett had noe issue, shee conferred her estate to Henrique, her husband's brother, whose daughter was married to John of Gant; and soe with the possessions of the Earldome of Lancaster the same[5] is come to the Crowne.

Secondlie, he shewed a paper crossed, purportinge that Richard Sampson, primo Julij, vicesimo octavo Hen: octavi, (the very daie of ye date of the graunt of the Inheritance to William Syliard and Eustace) had made a graunt of the same unto the then King's Matie.

His Matie's aunsweare to him was, 'If yow thincke it be of any validitie, give it to my Attorney.'

Att the last, my Lord Bishpp made a sewte to his Matie:—Inasmuch as Lincolne's Inne was in auncient time the London house of his predicessors, and they had formerlye more houses in London than all the Bishopps of England,—one of which was alsoe swallowed in the buildinge of Somersett House, as this was by the lawyers—and this was worth fifteene hundred pounds by the yere—that therefore he might have lodgings allowed him in the house of Lincolne's Inne, the Bishopps of his Sea not haveing a howse in London wherein to hide his head.

Mr Recorder saied that his Lord^p looked upon Lincolne's Inne, not as it was when it came from his Sea, but as it was att this time improved; affirminge that fortie thousand pownds had been bestowed upon it since y^t tyme.

His Matie demaunded, 'Have yow ever allowed any Bishopp lodgings?' The which was denyed by us.

His Matie withdrewe himselfe into his bedd chamber; and my Lord Bishopp, goeinge into the Gallery, staying there a good space with M^r

---

[1] Probably Hubert de Burgh, Earl of Kent.
[2] This is mistaken. See Ch. III.   [3] In 1276.   [4] Of Canterbury.
[5] I.e. the Inn.

Recorder and Mr Glanvill, declared himselfe in these termes:—'*Liberavi animam meam*; my successors should not blame me for not takinge care of the right of the Church'; and seemed satisfied with his Matie's determynacion.

Thus was the title of the Inn confirmed. No doubt the Bishop believed that the property had been sold to the Sulyards at an undervalue, as the result of intrigue in which King Henry VIII had been involved. This is the probable explanation of his attempt to recover it, and of his ejaculation at the end of it all—*Liberavi animam meam.* That King Henry VIII did concern himself with the transaction seems to be probable, because in the Chapter Act book of the Diocese of Chichester, a cancelled grant to the King immediately precedes the grant to the Sulyards.[1] But the Bishop, who produced no evidence in support of his allegations, revealed in the course of his arguments, not only a layman's natural ignorance of the subtleties of the law, but surprising ignorance of facts and documents; and there is no ground for supposing impropriety or undervalue. Bishop Sherborne had recently granted a new lease for ninety-nine years at an annual rent of ten marks (converted by the Bishop to £6. 13s. 4d.)[2] and the propriety of this lease was not challenged. Even allowing for the vast change in the value of money, this seems to have been a low rent, and was probably due to the dilapidations. £200, which the Sulyards paid, does not seem to be an unreasonable price for a reversion expectant upon a lease having more than ninety years to run at that small rent. That was in 1536. According to the Recorder, £40,000 had been spent upon the Inn between then and the hearing of this cause.

However this may be, those proceedings, interesting and exceptional though they were, shed no light on the story of the Inn before 1422. Its representatives were able to rely on its documents of title. No attempt was made to trace the history of the property back to the Black Friars, which was the prevailing view at the time. But modern research has proved conclusively that the Earl of Lincoln's House, which was built upon land which had once belonged to them, was not upon the site of Lincoln's Inn.

[1] B.B. IV. 286.   [2] *Ante*, pp. 19, 23.

CHAPTER III

THE BISHOP'S INN AND THE EARL'S INN

THE internal evidence provided by the earliest Black Book, together with modern research into the origins of the Inns of Court generally, leads irresistibly to the conclusion that Lincoln's Inn had been in existence for many years before 1422, and that it was by then a well-developed institution in full working order, already known as Lincoln's Inn.

The grounds for the conclusion may be shortly stated.

(1) The title of the first volume of the Black Books is not 'liber hospitii de Lincoln', but 'liber hospitii de Lincolns*in*'.

(2) The Black Books record no organic changes of constitution for a long time after 1422, and this suggests that the Society had already proved itself by experience. Moreover, they mention several practices which had already acquired the force of custom, and when every member took an oath to be '*obediens assistans et consortans* to the Governors in all things concerning the Society' he was probably not submitting himself to an absolute dictatorship, because a customary code confined the action of the Governors within recognized limits.[1]

(3) The first seven folios of the first Black Book comprise lists of ninety-six *socii* or fellows. After that come the names of students. All the *socii* must have been admitted before 1420, and the students 'keeping' their third Christmas cannot have been admitted later. Those ninety-six *socii* (all of them 'Masters') do not appear to have been original or founder members. If not, they must in their turn have been pupils of former Masters who had the right to train them and admit them to the order of 'Masters'. It is probable[2] that the Master certified that his pupils had attained a standard of legal education which entitled them to audience at the Bar of the Court (not to be confused with the Bar of the Inn). A number of such Masters of the Law, drawn by the ties of their common profession to live together in London, and taking, housing, educating and controlling pupils, would tend to assume an institutional form. As J. D. Walker

[1] B.B. I. Preface by J. D. Walker, p. xxxviii.
[2] See B.B. I. xxxix.

says in his introduction to the first printed volume of extracts from the Black Books:[1]

Thus originated the Society of Lincoln's Inn; a body of Masters of the Faculty of Law, giving lectures and instructing their pupils in law, and when satisfied of the proficiency of their pupils, admitting them to the order of Masters by calling them to the Bar, and further ... enforcing on the newly called an *inceptio* after the fashion of the great mediaeval Universities. It becomes at any rate possible to understand how Fortescue, Coke and Selden speak of the Inns of Court as universities for the study of the law on the same footing as the Universities of Oxford and Cambridge.

In assessing the historical value of Fortescue's description of the Inns, it is well to remember the title of his work. His praises seem to be too fulsome and lacking in discrimination. Yet his influence on early legal literature was marked.

Moreover, the use of the words 'certified' and 'lectures' in the foregoing extracts from Walker's Preface, withdrawn from their context, might inadvertently conjure up a picture of a system of legal education comparable with that now available. This would be a distorted picture. The methods of those days were rudimentary according to modern standards.

But two proved, or almost certain, facts are outstanding. The first is that even before 1422 the Inns of Court had acquired the exclusive privilege of qualifying persons to practise in the King's courts, and such a privilege could not in reason have been granted without an obligation to provide instruction and practical training in law up to the standards prevailing at the time. It is not known when or how the privilege came to them. But it was of long standing, and if it had come after 1422, the Black Books could hardly have failed to make mention of it.

The second of those facts is that a system of moots was in operation in Lincoln's Inn before 1422. This method of teaching by disputation, which was then in vogue, combines instruction in law with practice in advocacy, and accordingly has particular value in a course of practical training. It is a method still in use, and could be extended further with advantage. The first reference to moots in the Black Books is in 1428, when it was resolved that Robert Baynard should be expelled for disobedience and 'default in mooting'.[2] This turn of phrase suggests that the holding of moots had been a regular fea-

[1] *Ibid.* xl.   [2] *Ibid.* 3.

ture of the life of the Inn long enough for the word 'mooting' to be coined for it. Moreover if 'mooting' had been inaugurated between 1422 and 1427, some less oblique reference to the novelty would surely have been inevitable. It cannot be said with certainty that 'bolts' had been introduced before 1422. But they probably had. The distinction between moots and bolts is somewhat obscure. It may be that students took part in the argument in bolts, but not in moots.[1]

Terms were undoubtedly short; but every new member of the Inn was expected to be in residence (*continuer yci*) during three vacations for three years. These were the Easter, the Autumn or Michaelmas, and the Christmas vacations, which were known as 'learning vacations'. The periods of the year which were neither term nor learning vacations were called 'mesne vacations'.

On the eighth folio of the first Black Book is a list of thirty-one names headed *Ceux sont les nonns de ceux qe fueront assignes de continuer yci le nowel, l'an primer H.vj.* 'These are the names of those who were required to reside here at Christmas in the first year of Henry VI' (1422). To each name is added *pur soun primer, seconde* or *terce nowelle* (for his first, second or third Christmas), as the case may be.[2] The editors record that similar lists occur all through the volume. In 1442 the Easter vacation extended from the Vigil of Palm Sunday for three weeks following. The Autumn or Michaelmas vacation began a fortnight before the feast of Michaelmas and ended one week after it, and the Christmas vacation ran from the Vigil of Christmas to the morrow of Epiphany.[3] Walker states that the period of these vacations was the same in 1422.[4]

It is probable that moots and bolts were held in term as well as in the learning vacations even at this early date, though the elaborate provisions which are to be found in other volumes of the Black Books belong to a later date.

It is impossible to be certain whether 'readings', which were roughly equivalent to lectures, took place as early as 1422. The first mention of a Reader is in 1464, when it was ordered that in every year in future, the Autumn Reader should be elected in the previous Easter Term, and that the Lent Reader should be elected in the previous Michaelmas Term.[5] It is apparent from the form of this minute that the office of Reader was not being created then for the first time, but there is no evidence to show how long it had been in existence. Probably for a long time; because in 1502 a Lent Reader was fined for having given no Reading in the fourth week 'contrary to the ancient custom of the Society'.[1]

But whether or not Readings had been instituted before 1422, it seems to be clear that a system of instruction and training in law, designed to qualify students to practise in the courts, was then already in operation in Lincoln's Inn.

This conclusion was not accepted by Professor Thorne. In a lecture delivered in Gray's Inn in 1959,[2] he suggested by way of conjecture that 'it may even be said that the Society's move in 1422 from its former to its new quarters in Chancery Lane . . . was made to provide lodging for the students it had begun to enrol and those it expected to enrol in the future,' though he disclosed no evidence that the Society did in fact move in that year. He then said: 'but it is clear that in the years immediately following 1422 the procedures for educating these young men were first being worked out'.[3] Later he said: 'The great change in legal education came in Lincoln's Inn in 1442, though it was already in the air twenty years before, and several preliminary steps had already been taken.'[4]

His argument proceeded upon the footing that (1) the Society in 1422 consisted of 'distinguished and elderly members',[5] (2) the officers of the Society in the early fifteenth century were the Treasurer, the Pensioner, the Marshal, the collector of fuel money, the auditors of accounts and the collector of chapel money[6] (thereby apparently implying that there was no officer primarily concerned with education), (3) when in 1436 certain leading members of the Inn covenanted with the 'Fellowship' of Lincoln's Inn to 'continue' on certain days and parts of vacations, a preliminary step was taken[7] and (4) when in 1442 it was ordained by the Governors that every one who should thereafter be admitted to the Society should 'continue, every year, for the three years next after his admission, as follows, namely from the Vigil of Christmas to the morrow of the Epiphany, from the Vigil of Palm Sunday for three weeks following, and for the two weeks next before Michaelmas and the week after the same feast, and this under a penalty of 20s. for each default,[8] a great change came in legal education.

These arguments seem to merit criticism both in general and in

---

[1] *Ibid.* 125.   [2] Printed in *Graya*, no. 50 (1959), p. 79.   [3] P. 87.
[4] P. 91.   [5] P. 80.   [6] P. 81.   [7] P. 89. See B.B. I. 6.
[8] P. 91. See B.B. I. 12.

particular. In general, they overlook altogether the summary of the sequence of lists of compulsory attendances in vacations in the first volume of the Black Books which has already been quoted. It is thought that the accuracy of that summary, which has hitherto been recognized as authoritative, should only be displaced by further detailed research into the form and content of those lists which resulted in the discovery of some inaccuracy in it. On the other hand, if the summary is accepted, it seems to be imperative to accept the views of Walker, which are based mainly on the lists, in preference to a theory which takes no account of them.

With regard to the arguments in detail, if the first is intended to indicate that in 1422 there was an undue proportion of older men in the Inn, there is no known evidence to support this suggestion, which seems difficult to reconcile with the fact that some of those who 'continued' at Christmas 1422 were 'keeping' their first, second or third Christmas.

In connection with the second argument, it may be necessary to remember that in 1422, 1428 and 1442 (which are the critical years), the 'governance' of the Society was in the hands of Governors. The first mention of a Treasurer was in 1455,[1] and the first mention of a Reader was in 1464. But moots were undoubtedly held as early as 1428.

As regards the third argument, Walker suggested that the covenants were probably made to secure the attendance of seniors in vacations.[2] They cannot have been a preliminary step towards legal education, because compulsory attendance by junior members was required as early as 1422, and is expressly recognized in two of the covenants. Haye promised to fulfil the continuance 'that he is bound to, that is to wit, all the three vacations next coming' and in addition to make further continuances. Hillersdon promised to fulfil 'his said continuance due, that is to wit, on to Candlemas come a twelve month', and to make additional continuances.[3] The taking of these covenants appears to have been a step to fortify an already existing system.

As to the fourth argument, Walker evidently did not consider that the order of 1442 made any change at all, because the periods of the several vacations mentioned in it are the same as those which, in his view, prevailed in 1422. This entry in volume II of the Black Books may therefore merely represent a transfer from another book. It is

---

[1] B.B. I. 25.   [2] *Ibid.* xxv.   [3] *Ibid.* 6.

immediately followed by the remark: 'The other ordinances of the same Governors appear in the other Black Book of manucaptors.' On the other hand, the duration and dates of one or more of the vacations may have varied from time to time and the penalty certainly did so. But it made no change of substance or principle. This is apparent from the final provision of the order, which was that 'Every person who has already been admitted but has not continued for three years before this ordinance, according to custom, shall continue the remainder in form aforesaid and under the penalty aforesaid.'[1]

For these reasons it is thought right to adhere to the generally accepted view that already in 1422 a system of legal training was in operation in Lincoln's Inn, and that this is one of the grounds for holding that the Inn had an earlier history.

If this is so, it must be asked when, where and how did the Inn come into being? This question involves a short discussion of the origin of Inns of Court generally, because undoubtedly there was much that was common to all of them, both in their origin and in their activities. It must be admitted at the outset that there is no direct evidence. This has been pointed out by a long line of authors from Dugdale, through Pollock and Holdsworth, to Sir Cecil Carr in his recently published *Pension Book of Clement's Inn*. Indeed, perhaps Sir Cecil Carr is over-cautious, because after referring to the authenticated 'formative events' of the thirteenth century, he treats the rest as 'guess-work'.[2] For there is a tradition with a long history which has stood unchallenged until recently, and there are a number of established facts, from which reasonable inferences can be drawn, although the circumstantial evidence may not attain to the standard required for proof. Consideration of this type of evidence suggests that the foundation of the Inns of Court should be associated with the urge towards the study and teaching of law and the training of lawyers which had its first definite sign-post in 1292. The situation at that time has been described by Sir Frederick Pollock in the extract which follows from his address to the Canadian Guests of the Society in 1931.[3]

King Edward I is ruling with a firm hand... He is ruling much more than England; Aquitaine and Gascony are no mean compensation for Normandy. Foreign trade is increasing, Lombards and Flemings are introducing us to new methods of business. Our old popular courts of the

---

[1] *Ibid.* 12.   [2] P. xvi.   [3] *Ante*, p. 15.

D

county and the hundred, with their infrequent sittings, inflexibly formal procedure, and, what is even worse, lack of executive power, are in the eyes of merchants and traders effete for all practical purposes. Private courts of lords and customary local courts are good only for small matters. Men are eagerly seeking the king's justice, and need no longer seek it by toilsome and costly journeys, even beyond seas if the king is on an expedition abroad. The king's judges are at Westminster; he sends out his justices of assize into country parts; the clerks of his chancery are willing to help suitors—not for nothing, but willing just because it is to their profit—so far as the jealousy of the lords of manors and franchises for their privileges will allow them a free hand... Meanwhile the Church has forbidden clerks in orders to appear as advocates in secular courts. Therefore there must now be an order of learned laymen. The king has appointed such men to be his serjeants, *servientes ad legem*, not only for his own convenience but for his people's. But there are not very many of them, and there is need of younger pleaders to assist them in court and attend to matters of routine out of court; a sort of men who may hope, if they thrive, to become serjeants themselves in due time. Where shall we find the right sort?

That seems to have been the atmosphere in which King Edward I in 1292 made the Order in Council '*De attornatis et apprenticiis*' (a description which is believed to have included all court advocates below the rank of serjeant). This Order was addressed to John de Metingham, Chief Justice of the Common Pleas, and his *socii*, and its purpose[1] was to secure recruitment of an adequate number of apprentices (probably mainly, though not exclusively, from among the young pupils of the serjeants).

The major part of this important Order in Council was translated by Dugdale[2] in the following passage:

Id est—King Edw. I did especially appoint John de Metingham (then Lord Chief Justice of the Court of Common Pleas) and the rest of his fellow justices (of that court) that they, according to their discretions, should provide and ordain, from every county, certain attorneys and lawyers of the best and most apt for their learning and skill, who might do service to his Court and people; and that those, so chosen only, and no other should follow his court, and transact the affairs therein... So that soon afterwards, though we have no memorial of the direct time, nor absolute certainty of the places, we may safely conclude that they settled in certain hostels or Inns, which were thenceforth called 'Inns of Court'.

[1] Pollock, *ibid*. See also Holdsworth, *History of English Law*, 3rd edn. II. 314.
[2] *Origines Juridiciales*, p. 141.

It is not known what steps were taken by the Chief Justice, or his *socii*, or others to implement this Order (although it is almost certain that the Earl of Lincoln played an important part),[1] but it seems to have set on foot the movement which led to the foundation of the many Inns which have not survived, and the four which have. This was certainly Dugdale's view.

This indeed has for a long time been the generally accepted view, and Holdsworth was particularly emphatic in accepting it. When reviewing Williams' Book in *The Law Quarterly Review*, he wrote:

It may be true to say that the idea that the Inns of Court and Chancery were a university of English law was a deduction from the position which they had attained in the 15th and 16th centuries; but it was a legitimate deduction, and having regard to Fortescue and other authorities, it is, I think, definitely wrong to maintain that the Inns of Court and Chancery had no obligations in connexion with legal education. Legal education was in fact their principal raison d'être.[2]

This view has been challenged by Professor Thorne in the lecture in Gray's Inn to which reference has already been made. He then said: 'But it is much more likely that at the Inns . . . teaching duties were only slowly grafted on to older institutions in which they had originally played no part. . .'[3]

Three proved facts have to be taken into account in drawing inferences about the origins of the Inns which have sufficient validity to be regarded as reasonable. The first, to which reference has already been made,[4] is that from a remote past the Inns have between them enjoyed an exclusive privilege of qualifying their members to practise in the courts. It is a necessary inference that this privilege must have been granted, or acquiesced in, by the Sovereign, either directly, or acting through high officers of State. These would be probably, but not necessarily, the Judges, either of their own initiative, or at the request of the King, or one of his Ministers. In the Preface to volume II of the Black Books, Walker wrote: 'the Judges . . . had the power of prescribing what persons should practise as advocates in their courts. It would seem that the exercise of this power must have followed close on the first appearance of advocates, and prior to the earliest origins of the Inns of Court.'[5]

The second, to which some reference has also been made,[6] is that

---

[1] See Ch. V.   [2] Vol. XLIV (1928), p. 386.   [3] *Graya*, no. 50 (1959), p. 87.
[4] *Ante*, p. 29.   [5] B.B. II. xxxvi.   [6] *Ante*, p. 29.

some legal training was in fact provided by the Inns from a date which is earlier than the written records, and it seems reasonable to infer that the provision of such training was an essential prerequisite for the exclusive privilege. This is Walker's view,[1] and the Judges certainly exercised without any challenge some supervision over the education provided in the seventeenth century.

The third is that the Judges have intervened without any question being raised, whenever they have thought such a course to be desirable. Nowadays they remain Benchers in the Inn, or one of the Inns, to which they belonged before appointment, and their influence is normally exercised individually, and without formality, there. But there is one power which they still exercise when occasion requires —the power, on hearing an appeal by a disbarred member, to order his reinstatement if they think proper. They probably still have other powers, but they have not found it necessary to assert them for a long time past. But this was not the case in the seventeenth century.

A striking example occurred in 1627–8, when the Judges, after making a number of orders about Readers, made orders that all Readers, Benchers, Barristers, and other Students and Fellows in every House of Court and Chancery, should repair to the hall at dinner, supper and exercises, in their caps and not in hats; and should likewise repair to the church, chapel and place of prayer in their caps; and that they should not come with boots. They further ordered that such Reader as should contemptuously break any of the orders aforesaid should not be suffered to practise at any Bar at Westminster, or at the Assizes.[2] These orders were presented to the Masters of the Bench on 29 January 1628, and accepted without any recorded comment. They were ordered to be transcribed and screened 'to the end that the gentlemen of this Society may take notice thereof'.[3]

The generally accepted theory takes account of all these special features, and has a historical background. It would be remarkable if all this was mere coincidence. It may fairly be said therefore that there is circumstantial evidence for it which approximates to proof. Some criticism of Professor Thorne's theory of the late introduction of legal education in Lincoln's Inn has already been made. It would be premature to discuss his major proposition that teaching duties originally played no part, until he has provided his explanation on

[1] B.B. II. xxxvii.   [2] *Ibid.* 451.   [3] *Ibid.* 275.

that basis of the three special features. But although teaching of law and the training of lawyers are thought to have been the primary function, it may be conceded at once that it was not their only function. These hostels were convenient and desirable places of meeting for all engaged in the profession of the law, especially for those whose only business in London was during the short terms; and whether or not it was originally contemplated that they should become focal points for the discussion of professional matters and the advancement of professional interests, they naturally became so in the result.

These other activities are stressed in the hitherto unpublished account of the origin of the Inns given by the author of the *M.T.MS.* who includes, but does not emphasize, the educational purpose. It is as follows:

The common laws of England fairly flourished in the peaceable times of the three first Edwards, kings here, and so did the professors of our laws. For after that the Court of Common pleas became severed from other courts of justice that followed the King's Court, and was established unto a place certain, which was (as may be well conjectured) about the King's Palace at Westminster, then did the reverent judges, serjeants-at-law and other learned 'legists' begin to settle themselves also to meet and convenient places to consolidate and cohabit in, as well for ease as decency, as also the better and more free access of the subject to advise and thereupon to receive justice when it was required, and for that purpose they grew into sundry associations, and they severed themselves into several collegial places, where they might at meet and convenient times, as well in the term times as otherwise, converse, confer and consolidate together. And these superior professors of the laws, having planted themselves in several situations, by their laudable example, others of a more mean profession (yet desiring to taste of the breast milk offered from that nursery) did likewise in process of time make divers particular assemblies, and therewith betook themselves to several residing places, there to study, confer and converse together, as members of one united Society. And the greatest number of these inferiors were at the first merely students of the municipal or common laws, and in ensuing times the number of them decreased and professed to be Agents and Solicitors for their neighbour countrymen, near hand and further remote from this Academy. But before such time as the supreme society had confined themselves and their studies to those Houses or Inns or Court, namely the two Temples, and those of Lincoln's and Gray's Inn, all or a great number of them kept 'hospitality' here and there, every one as to himself best seemed, whereof this house of Thavies Inn was a primary place of residence, Clifford Inn another with sundry others, as those then in those days in or near St. 'Sepulcher's' Church,[1] called St. George's Inn, another Scrope's Inn, Paternoster Row, and another in some obscure place within or near unto Dowgate, called Johnson's Inn, or the now Stillyard near London Bridge, and these inferior houses, being replenished with competent numbers professing the law, were entitled Inns of Chancery, and were of none other condition than Halls are to Colleges in the Universities of Oxford and Cambridge, as in very deed they so were and are to these Colleges or Houses of Court, and are become (as best beseemeth) members thereof, to whom withal is appropriate a government supreme, to direct and correct, as to a superior power appertaineth.[2]

While it is permissible to attribute with confidence the foundation of the Inns of Court generally to those times and circumstances, is it possible to be more specific about the origin of Lincoln's Inn? The ancient tradition was as simple as it was venerable. It was that Henry de Lacy, Earl of Lincoln, founded the Society about 1300 and established it in its present home. This was supposed by Stow and later writers to have been his London residence. Unfortunately for this theory, however, modern research has shown that his residence was on another site near Shoe Lane. It has also established (as has already been mentioned) that there was another Inn in the neighbourhood, actually named 'Lincoln's Inn', which belonged to Thomas de Lincoln, a serjeant-at-law, and was probably at one time conducted by him as a hostel for law students. Naturally enough, therefore, some have sought to substitute the Serjeant for the Earl as the founder of the Society. But, as will emerge in Chapter VI, there are serious objections to this theory, founded on reason no less than on sentiment; and it may well be that the ancient tradition is not so seriously discredited as might have been expected. It may therefore be of interest to restate it as recounted in Sulyard's newly discovered and earlier record, to analyse it as recorded there and by other writers, and then to consider how far the new evidence which has been made available during the last sixty years tends to confirm or reject it.

Sulyard's account, as extracted by the author of the *M.T.MS.*, was as follows:[3]

He (Sulyard) also relateth that in the reigns of K. Edw. I and of K. Edw. II Hen. Lacy Earl of Lincoln and Lord High Steward of England to which [saith Mr. Sulyard] appertained immediately under the King the

---

[1] In Seacoal Lane, near Newgate.   [2] Fos. 79–79d.   [3] Fo. 2d.

sole administration of justice, and to have a due respect unto the execution of the same. And therefore [saith he] all ministers and students of the law bare to him an obedience. By whose wisdom and policy, companies were gathered into places to study the laws of this realm, there to cohabit together, under honest rules and orders. And the said Earl, as of old time [saith he] by tradition and by the Ancients of this Society is reported, brought a company to this House being at that time very ruinous and out of repair which company [saith he] hath continued the space of 240 years etc. . . and the company [saith he] was brought hither by the Earl of Lincoln and this House by the said Earl provided for them. And thereby assumed the name of Lincoln's Inn. And that [saith he] bears likelihood of truth. For that the Arms of Earl Lacy, being Or, a lion rampant purple, hath been always since set up in this House in memory thereof.

Indeed, Sulyard himself set them upon the new gatehouse.[1]

The contrast between his unqualified statement of the connection of the Earl with the foundation of Inns of Court in general and his tentative acceptance of the traditional story of Lincoln's Inn is noticeable. It is surprising that the Ancients, whose memories must have stretched back well into the fifteenth century, should have been so vague about the origins of the Society, and had never heard of Thomas de Lincoln's Inn. But though the early tradition, as recorded by Sulyard, was that the Earl himself brought the Society to its present home, and it knew nothing about migrations, it did not assert that the house which was described as being 'very ruinous and out of repair', was the Earl's own house. This theory first appears in Stow's Survey in 1598. He wrote:[2]

On the west side of New Street [later known as Chancery Lane] towards the north end thereof was (of old time) the church and house of the Preaching [Black] Friars. . . These Friars came to London, and had their first house without the wall of the city by Oldbourne near unto Old Temple[3]. . . This old Friar-house (juxta Holbourn, saith the Patent) was by King Edward I in the 16th year of his reign given to Henry Lacy, Earl of Lincoln. Next to this house of Friars was one other great House, sometime belonging to the Bishop of Chichester. . . In this place after the decease of the said Bishop (1244) and in the place of the house of Black Friars before spoken of, Henry Lacy, Earl of Lincoln, Constable of

---

[1] In 1552 a lantern was set up on the (old) Hall (B.B. I. 302) 'on the outside whereof' wrote Dugdale in 1666 (p. 232) 'in lead the armes of Lacy Earl of Lincoln with Quincy and the Earl of Chester's cote are still to be seen'.

[2] These passages are cited in B.B. IV. 263.

[3] Not to be confused with the Temple south of Fleet Street.

Chester and Custos of England built his Inn and for the most part lodged there.

The same theory was propounded by Francis Thynne, and later writers, and was generally accepted until 1904.

But W. P. Baildon, in his essay on the site of the Inn,[1] has convincingly demonstrated that the Earl's house (which certainly had belonged to the Black Friars) was not in Chancery Lane, but at the north-east corner of Shoe Lane;[2] and that the house of the Bishop in which the Inn settled had never belonged to the Earl.

Turner, who was at work on the history of Lincoln's Inn as early as 1903, was not then inclined to accept the view that the Earl had never owned an Inn on the present site, and observed:

Its name, however, supplies some evidence of its ownership ... we should expect to find that Lincoln's Inn once belonged to the earls or bishops of Lincoln, it being too large a building to be the inn of a commoner. We certainly ought not to believe that it took its name from an Earl of Lincoln who was neither its owner nor its occupier, unless some instances of a like adoption of a name can be adduced. The tradition of the Inn is that it belonged to Henry de Lacy, Earl of Lincoln, and there is very little reason for doubting that the tradition is in substance correct.[3]

A few pages later he wrote:

If we suppose that the Inn was formerly the property of the earls of Lincoln, that it passed from them to the Hospitallers, and from the Hospitallers to Robert Stratford, bishop of Chichester by a conveyance dated about the year 1339, we shall have no stronger reason for supposing that the tenancy of the lawyers began under the bishops than under the Hospitallers.[4]

But in spite of Turner's arguments to the contrary, there seems to be no doubt about the Bishop's Inn or his title. It had once formed part of the estate of John Herlycun or Herlizun which was forfeited to King Henry III and was by him granted to Ralph Neville, Bishop of Chichester in 1226–7.[5] The original charter is in the possession of the Society. Probably soon afterwards the Bishop began to build, and *ibidem sumptuose edificavit*.[6] Of this building only fragments, probably of a window, remain. They were dug up when the Chapel was extended westward in 1877, and show (according to Baildon) that the palace was in the early English style of architecture.[7] The

[1] B.B. IV. 263.   [2] *Ibid.* 266.   [3] 'Lincoln's Inn' (a pamphlet), (1903), p. 17.
[4] *Ibid.* p. 21.   [5] B.B. IV. 279.   [6] *Ibid.* 280.   [7] *Ibid.* 280.

Bishop died there in 1244, as is recorded in the *M.T.MS*[1] and elsewhere.

Bishop Neville was succeeded by Bishop Richard who died in 1253. He was afterwards canonized and known as St Richard of Chichester. The chapel was dedicated to him, and his image was placed there.[2]

It is most unfortunate that, owing to the destruction of the early Registers of the Bishops in 1642,[3] it is impossible to state definitely whether any of Bishop Neville's successors actually resided in his palace, and if so, when they ceased to do so, and whether they occupied the whole or a part only. There is a good deal of evidence that they had an office there. When on 12 July 1340 Robert de Stratford, Bishop of Chichester, was sworn in on appointment as Chancellor for the second time, the Close Roll, in recording the ceremony, refers to the Bishop's 'chamber' ('camera') in his Inn.[4] The Close Roll of 1375 refers to Ficketts Field 'adjoining the Bishop of Chichester's Inn'. But, as Turner long ago pointed out, such a description 'implies ownership but not necessarily residence' and certainly not 'exclusive occupation'.[5] The same may be said of the references in Bishop Reade's Register (1396–1415) to documents *datum in hospitio nostro London*'.[6] It is quite possible that the Bishop's staff had over a long period of years shared the accommodation in the palace with the lawyers, though they did not do so later than 1422. It is also possible (as Turner suggests)—indeed probable—that during the earlier period of the Inn's occupation the Bishop himself lodged there when the business of his see or of the State brought him to London. Bishop Montague contended in the proceedings at Whitehall in 1635 that 'divers of his predecessors had . . . reserved lodgings in the Howse when they should repayre to London aboute their owne busines or his Majesty's affairs'.[7] He produced no evidence to substantiate his claim, and there was no such reservation in Bishop Sherborne's lease to William Sulyard in 1535, nor any record of any such happening in the Black Books. The representatives of the Society had therefore no means of knowing, and their denial to the King was no doubt made in good faith. But such an arrangement would not be surprising in the circumstances of the time, and it is significant that when the Abbot of Malmesbury assigned his 'Lyncolnesynne' to charitable uses in 1383 he reserved the use of

---

[1] *Ante*, p. 12.   [2] B.B. I. 41, 313.   [3] B.B. IV. 281.   [4] *Ibid.* 281.
[5] *Op. cit.* p. 21.   [6] B.B. IV. 283.   [7] *Ante*, p. 23.

the new Inn to himself and his successors 'when in London for the Parliament of the King or other business',[1] and a similar reservation was made by the monastery in a lease as late as 1525.[2]

There is therefore no evidence of the date when the lawyers first went to reside in the Bishop's Inn, and no sufficient basis for making any assumption about it. It could even have been in the lifetime of the Earl himself.

The Earl of Lincoln's own Inn was at the north-east corner of Shoe Lane. There is evidence that it was once so called, but its name was later changed to 'Strange's Inn'. Williams unearthed a document in which it is described in 1417 as 'the manor or Inn called "Straungesyn" and anciently (*ab antiquo*) called the manor or Inn of the Earl of Lincoln'.[3] Obviously this would soon be abbreviated into 'Lincoln's Inn'. Moreover, it is reasonable to suppose that it continued to be so called after the Earl's death, because it could not have acquired the name of 'Strange's Inn' before 1322. The Earl's heir was his daughter Alesia or Alice, and between 1322 and 1325 she married Ebulo or Ebulus le Strange, younger son of John, first Lord Strange of Knockyn,[4] and it was in this way that the name 'Strange' became associated with that Inn. It was not long afterwards that the name 'Lincoln's Inn' became associated with another property in the neighbourhood.[5]

Having regard to the Earl's close connection with legal administration,[6] it would not be surprising if he established a body of lawyers in his Inn; but there is no evidence that there were any lawyers there, either during his lifetime or before the Inn became known as Strange's Inn. But there is some evidence that there were lawyers in Strange's Inn in 1415. A record on the King's Bench Rolls describes a person as 'falsely claiming to be an apprentice of the law in Straungesyn'.[7] Even so, however, there is no other record of this group of lawyers before or afterwards, and no evidence at all that they migrated.

Faced with these problems, Baildon, who did not then know anything of Thomas de Lincoln's Inn, advanced the theory that the Society had been settled at John Thavy's house by the Earl of Lincoln, and had then moved from there to 'Lord Furnival's House', and finally migrated from there to the Bishop's Inn. This

[1] *Post*, p. 46.   [2] *Post*, p. 51.
[3] Hustings Rolls, 145, no. 28. W.D. no. 733.   [4] B.B. IV. 270.
[5] See Ch. IV.   [6] See Ch. V.   [7] W.D. no. 732.

theory he elaborated in volume IV of the Black Books.[1] It is based
upon the facts that Thavie's Inn had an entrance in Shoe Lane oppo-
site the Earl's house, that Furnival's Inn (which stood where the
Prudential Building now stands, but was demolished in 1897) did
become an Inn for lawyers, and that both had close associations
with Lincoln's Inn. Thavie's Inn may have been occupied by lawyers as early as 1348, though this is doubtful. It is mentioned in the
Black Books in 1482. Lincoln's Inn appointed the Readers at both
those Inns, and supervised them. It purchased the freehold of both
of them between 1548 and 1551. But there seem to have been many
legal societies in the neighbourhood, and now there is material in
the *M.T.MS.* which seems to undermine the foundations of Baildon's theory.

Of Furnival's Inn Dugdale wrote: 'This being long ago an house
of the Lord Furnivalls had thereupon the name of Furnivalls Inne,
and by some of them was antiently demised to the students of the
law; for in 9 H 4 (1407) it appears by their Steward's accompts that
they resided in it.'[2] This passage was known to, and indeed quoted
by, Baildon,[3] but he had not then seen any extracts from those accounts. He cited good evidence to show that the last Lord Furnival
to own the Inn was the fourth baron who died in 1383, and he suggests (as is probable) that he had purchased it from Roger atte Bogh.
On Lord Furnival's death the property was delivered up to his
daughter and heir Joan, the wife of Thomas de Neville, who became tenant by courtesy until his death in 1407, the year in which
the Steward's accounts open. Baildon suggested (and it is likely)
that law students had occupied the Inn since before 1383. It is easy
to infer from the accounts that their Society was not new in 1407,
but was already an established institution, closely resembling other
legal Inns. But his theory of a migration from that Inn to the Bishop's
Inn cannot be reconciled with the detail of the accounts which has
come to light in the *M.T.MS.*

Baildon wrote:

the Society, if my theory be right, does not seem to have been long at
Lord Furnival's house. . . I suggest that the same Society moved from
Furnival's house into the still more roomy Palace of the Bishops of
Chichester in Chancery Lane. . . This would be between the death of
Bishop Reade in 1415 and the commencement of the Black Books in
1422 . . . there is no evidence of the house of the Furnivals being called

[1] P. 293.   [2] *Op. cit.* p. 270.   [3] B.B. IV. 288.

Furnival's Inn until after the Society of Lincoln's Inn had (on my theory) left it.[1]

This last statement is no longer true, because the first extract from the accounts in the *M.T.MS.* is headed 'Furnivall's Inne 1407'.[2] The figures which can be extracted from these accounts also eliminate the possibility of any substantial migration between 1407 and 1422.

In 1407, 26 took commons on Christmas Day, and in the Hilary term the numbers in commons ranged from 70 to 58. This appears from a quoted extract, and the author comments: 'a like number of commoners continued together the four next ensuing years' (1408–11). In 1411 there appear to have been 83 in commons in the second week before Michaelmas and 58 in the week before Christmas. The author then remarks: 'in anno 1, 2, 3, H V like observations as before'. There were 72 in commons in the Hilary term of the following year. In 5 H V the numbers ranged between 73 and 57 and 32 took commons on Christmas Day. Then comes a gap until his death. But a new steward's account, extracted from a lost 'Black Book' of Furnival's Inn, begins with the new reign in 1422, the year in which the Lincoln's Inn Black Books also begin, and it shows that 43 took commons on Christmas Day.

If there had been a substantial exodus between 1407 and 1422, it would necessarily have been revealed in a sudden fall in attendances and otherwise in these accounts. As they only begin in 1407, they do not of necessity preclude the possibility of an earlier exodus. But Baildon did not suggest this, and any such suggestion would be improbable.

[1] B.B. IV. 295.   [2] Fo. 83.

CHAPTER IV

THOMAS DE LINCOLN'S INN

BUT a more serious theory sprang up with the rediscovery of
Thomas de Lincoln's Inn—more serious because it seeks to de-
throne the Earl as founder. The researches of the late G. J. Turner
of Lincoln's Inn and of the late E. Williams, F.R.G.S., conclusively
prove that there was another Lincoln's Inn, east of Staple Inn and
south of Holborn, which derived its name from Thomas de Lincoln,
a serjeant-at-law who practised in the Court of Common Pleas.[1] He
began to acquire this property in 1331, when he bought the tenement of John de Chester. It consisted of a messuage with two shops
and a garden; it had a frontage of about thirty-three feet along the
'Holebourne' highway, and was situated between the tenement of
Robert le Hende towards the west and the tenement of Robert le
Goldsmith and Andrew Coupere towards the east; and it extended
southwards for no less than about 625 feet as far as the Chancellor's
Ditch, which ran about seventy feet south of the present Cursitor
Street, and then formed the boundary between John de Chester's
tenement and a tenement of the Bishop of Chichester.[2] It was then
subject to a quit rent; but the Serjeant acquired the overlordship in
1348–9.[3] In 1332 he had purchased the gardens behind Robert le
Goldsmith's tenement and behind the three tenements to the east
of it, and this seems to have brought him as far as Fetter Lane.[4] In
1334 he bought the land and garden which constituted Robert le
Hende's tenement;[5] and when he sold the whole property, it consisted of three messuages and spacious grounds known as the
'Great Garden'.[6] It would be but natural that the Serjeant should
have had a number of law students in residence with him, and indeed Williams brought to light a small piece of documentary evidence to support this probability. It appears from the Coroner's
Rolls for the City of the year 1339[7] that an inquest was held
upon the death of two clerks of Chancery who suffered a violent

---

[1] See Law Pamphlets, vol. 267, in Lincoln's Inn Library (incorporating a photo-
stat extract from an article in the *Athenaeum* dated 22 September 1906) and
Early Holborn.

[2] W.D. no. 1117.   [3] W.D. no. 1127.   [4] W.D. nos. 1101, 1124.
[5] W.D. no. 1124.   [6] W.D. no. 1134.   [7] W.D. no. 1081.

death 'in the rent of Thomas de Lyncoln, pleader, in the parish of St. Andrew, Holborne' after being assaulted by four apprentices of the law. But there is some slight evidence that the Serjeant had retired and left the Inn by 1364,[1] and he certainly retired before May 1369.

On 1 May 1369 the property was assigned to the Abbot and Convent of Malmesbury.[2] Between then and 1383 the monastery acquired some adjoining property, and in particular the tenements of Gaillard Pete (sometimes called 'Pet, Poet or Port') on the east side and Walter Barton on the west. In 1383 the Abbot formally devoted the property to charitable uses. The parcels in this charter (translated) were as follows:

The whole of our Inn called 'Lyncolnesynne' in the parish of St. Andrew in Holborn in the suburb of London with all etc. and with the reversion of one messuage and one yard which Gaillard Pet and Agnes his wife hold until the end of their lives situate in the eastern part of our aforesaid Inn.

Williams discovered a letter written by the Abbot to the Pope on 6 October 1380[2] which throws much light on the position. He states that he and his Convent in Chapter have assigned to the Chapel of St Mary for the lights and repair of that chapel the Inn called 'Lyncolnesynne' 'provided that the Abbot and his successors when in London for the Parliament of the King or other business have the use and easement of their new inn newly built, next the great garden, and also the kitchen on the west side of the inn with free entrance and exit so that the Warden of the said Chapel shall at other times have free disposal of the said inn and kitchen'. There is a reference in the letter to 'the amounts to be given to monks for the time being in the Infirmary'.

This reference to the Abbot's 'new inn newly built, next the great garden' is important in connection with a theory which has been built up upon the foundation of a rent roll of the property dated 1399. This rent roll was found in a folio[3] of the chartulary of the Abbey of Malmesbury which is now in the Cotton Collection in the British Museum. The more significant entries are in a note, which is a later addition. It is difficult to read, and part is missing, because the bottom of the folio has been shaved off. It is in deciphering and interpreting the obscure entries that the Abbot's letter

---

[1] W.D. no. 1128.   [2] W.D. no. 1134.   [3] Faustina B. viii. fo. 253.

PLATE I. *M.T.M.S.*, fos. 5d and 6. Rent roll, and description of the old hall and the chapel of Lincoln's Inn

and also a newly discovered version of the rent roll which is embodied in the *M.T.MS.*[1] give so much help.

It is there introduced as follows:

In an old ancient manuscript book, remaining in the custody of Richard Digges Esquire late one of the Benchers of Lincoln's Inn and now Serjeant-at-law, is a ledger book which (as it seemeth) sometime belonged to the Abbey of St. Aldeline and of St. Augustine in Malmesbury and to St. Mary's chapel there.

This is a transcription of it.

Reddituale Capellae Beatae Mariae ibidem renovat(ae) tempore Johannis Rodburne tum custodis ibidem in festo Sanctae Barnabae Apostoli Anno Domini 1399.
De firmariis Novi Hospitii apud Londinium vocati Lincolnesynne ad quatuor terminos solut per annum 8^{li} pro missa Abbatis

And after thus:

De tenementis quondam Gaillard Port in Holborne xx^s
De tenementis quondam Walteri Bartone allucarii xiii^s iiii^d
Hospitium Armigeri q^x (?) magnum Hospitium quod est ruinosum redd. per annum xl^s.
Celda[2] prox. annexa Hosp. redd. per annum ix^s.
Secunda celda redd. per annum x^s
Tertia celda redd. per ann. viii^s.
Quarta celda que est fabrica redd. per annum xx^s.
Summa per annum 4^{li} 7^s ultr. redd. Magni Hospitii. Et ultr. redd. ten. Gaillard Port quod tenet Oliva relicta ejusdem. Et ultr. ten. Walteri Bartone quod tenet Relicta ejus.

There is an illegible marginal note in the *M.T.MS.* beside the words *De firmariis Novi Hospitii*, and a partially defaced marginal note adjoins the words *Hospitium Armigeri* which reads as follows:

---

[1] Fo. 5d. Fos. 5d and 6 are here reproduced by kind permission of the Honourable Society of the Middle Temple. Fo. 5d begins with the concluding words of an account of Lincoln's Inn in 1422. Then comes the rent roll; and after that, a description of the old hall and the Chapel.

[2] *Celda* is what is written in both manuscripts. But such a word is not to be found in any dictionary of classical latin, or in Baxter and Johnson (*Medieval Latin Word List*) or in *Lexicon manuale ad scriptores mediae et infimae Latinitatis* (Paris, 1866). It may be a mistake for, or corruption of, *cella*, which in a medieval document might be expected to mean a monastic cell. These small booths (the *Lexicon* uses the description *domuncula*) may have been monastic in origin. But they were not so used at this time. One of them was a *fabrica* or forge. The meaning of 'hut' or 'booth' is well authenticated from classical sources.

London . . . a tenentium . . . firmam Magni Hospitii. Part of one word
and the whole of another are missing from this note. But the word
firmam is absolutely clear.

The passage beginning *Hospitium Armigeri* and the marginal
note beside it were written at a later date and by a different scribe.
The chartulary makes this clear, although the *M.T.MS.* gives no
indication of it. The word *firmam* appears in both versions; but the
word which preceded it is missing from the *M.T.MS* version, and
is obscure in the chartulary. Mr S. J. Arthur, of the Manuscript
Department of the British Museum, kindly studied the marginal
note there for me, and reached the conclusion that the word was
infra. Accordingly it seems justifiable to treat *infra* as the word
missing from the *M.T.MS.* and to insert it before the clear word
firmam. Odgers, who read the note in the margin as *Tenura tenen-
cium infra silvam magni hospitii,*[1] also adopted *infra,* but substituted
silvam for *firmam,* and for this there is no warrant. Accordingly the
marginal note should read *tenura tenentium infra firmam Magni
Hospitii.* Williams translated it as 'Tenure of the tenants in the farm
in the great inn'.[2] It would seem therefore that he must have read
in firma, or words to that effect.

In both versions there is an obscure symbol in the text between
the words *Hospitium Armigeri* and the words *magnum hospitium.*
Odgers read it as *jam,* and attached much weight to it.[3] But Williams
did not so read it, to judge from his published translation, which is
'The Inn of the Esquire in the Great Inn which is dilapidated'.[4] It
may, however, be said with certainty that the symbol is neither
jam nor *in.* Mr Arthur has suggested that the symbol in the chartulary is an abbreviation for *infra,* and this may well be so. But in that
case the originator of the *M.T.MS.* copy must have failed to decipher it, because his version of it could not be read as *infra.* It looks
like 'q^x'. This may indicate a query. Or again, it may be an abbreviation for *que est,* a phrase which follows almost immediately in the
sentence *celda que est fabrica.* Fortunately this problem is not fundamental, although its solution would have thrown light on the ap-
proximate situations of the two inns, because if the symbol is *infra,*
the words *magnum hospitium* had by the date of the note come to
designate the Abbot's 'new' Inn, whereas if *que est* is read, that description still adhered to the ruined Serjeant's Inn.

---

[1] *Essays in Legal History*, p. 252.   [2] W.D. no. 1155.   [3] *Post*, p. 55.
[4] W.D. no. 1155.

It seems clear that the author of the *M.T.MS.* was right in placing the chapel of St Mary in Malmesbury, and that Williams[1] was wrong in thinking that it was in Lincoln's Inn. The Pope, in a letter to the Archbishop of Canterbury,[2] said that he understood that the Abbot had acquired property 'for the maintenance of lights in the chapel of St Mary in the Church of the monastery' and there is nowhere any hint that this was a misunderstanding. On the contrary, in a lease made in 1525–6, the Warden of the Chapel is referred to as the Warden of the 'Chapel of the Holy Virgin in the monastery aforesaid'.[3] The Pope's letter also seems to show that the infirmary which is mentioned in the Abbot's letter was the infirmary at Malmesbury. There is in fact no reason to suppose that the Convent bought the Serjeant's property, or built the new Inn, for their own permanent occupation, or for any monastic purpose. The warden of the Chapel, and not the Abbot, was to have the free disposition of the Inn and kitchen, subject to use by the Abbot when in London for business.

These are relevant factors in translating the word *firmariis* which appears in the *M.T.MS.* version of the rent roll, or *firmario* (sic), which occurs in the chartulary in the British Museum. If there had been an infirmary or infirmaries in the Inn, it might have referred to them. But it probably means 'renters'. It could mean 'farmers', but its translation must not be coloured by the word *firmam* in the marginal note, because it was written later by a different scribe.

Williams is thought to have been right in translating the word *firmam* in the marginal note as 'farm'. This would seem to be the primary meaning of the phrase *infra firmam*. It is true that at that period the word *firma* was also used to describe a fixed rent, or property rented, without any implication as to the use of the property. But in this case the rental unit was the *magnum hospitium*, whether or not that phrase included the Abbot's Inn, and the properties constituting that unit were only 'below' one another in a geographical sense. The translation of the word *firma* has some importance, because there is known to have been a 'farm of Lincoln's Inn', and although there is no corroboration that it was on this site, it may have been.

---

[1] *Post*, p. 53.   [2] Summarized in W.D. no. 1134.
[3] *Post*, p. 51. Moreover there is a reference in W.D. no. 1131 to the finding of six wax lights burning daily in the Abbey Church at the Mass of the Blessed Mary.

E

In the light of these preliminary observations the *M.T.MS.* version of the document may be translated as follows:

Rent Roll of the chapel of St Mary there,[1] restored in the time of John Rodburne then warden there at the festival of St. Barnabas the Apostle in the year of the Lord 1399.

> From the renters of the new inn in London called 'Lincoln's Inn', payable at four quarter days—£8 per annum (for the Abbot's Mass)
> From the tenements formerly of Gaillard Port in Holborn—20/-
> From the tenements formerly of Walter Barton, cordwainer—13/4
> The Inn of the Serjeant[2] below the great inn (or in the alternative, which is the great inn) which is ruinous, payable 40/- per annum
> The booth nearby attached to the Inn payable per annum 9/-
> The second booth, payable per annum—10/-
> The third booth, payable per annum—8/-
> The fourth booth which is a forge, payable per annum—20/-
> Total per annum payable in addition for the great Inn—£4.7.0. And in addition the rent of Gaillard Port's tenement of which his widow Olive is tenant. And in addition the rent of Walter Barton's tenement which his widow holds.

The marginal note beside the words *Hospitium Armigeri* may be translated: 'tenure of the tenants below the farm of the Great Inn'.

Though the rent roll is dated 1399, and the entry relating to the Abbot's 'new' Inn was presumably made in that year, all the entries referring to the *magnum hospitium* were made later. But perhaps not much later, because the widows of Port and Barton, albeit second wives, were alive when the additional entries were made. But much more important than the actual date of these is the overall picture given by the rent roll as a whole; and, in spite of doubts affecting some matters of detail, its main features are clear. The Abbot's letter had already created an expectation that there would be two Inns on the property, his newly built Inn and the Serjeant's old Inn. The rent roll fulfils this expectation.

(1) There is the Abbot's new Inn, built by the monastery between 1369 and 1380, and rented by sundry tenants at rents amounting in all to £8 per annum.

(2) There is what is described in the added marginal note as being 'below the farm of the great inn'. This seems to have been the rest of

[1] I.e. at Malmesbury.
[2] The word means 'Esquire'. But Odgers and Williams agree that it should be translated 'Serjeant', and this seems to be correct.

the property bought from the Serjeant, and at the date of the addition it consisted of his Inn, which was ruinous, and was rented for £2 per annum only, and four booths which brought in a higher rent, namely £2. 7s. od. per annum between them.

(3) There are the tenements associated with the names of Port and Barton, which had never belonged to the Serjeant.

(4) Unfortunately the 'great garden' is not expressly mentioned in the roll, and the farm has neither a tenant nor a rent specifically assigned to it. But is seems to be a reasonable assumption that the greater part of the garden had been incorporated in the farm before the roll assumed its final form.

(5) All these properties were at that date still known as Lincoln's Inn.

This is the last indisputable reference to these properties under that name.

Williams thought that there was evidence that the whole property was known as 'Lincoln's Inn' in 1417. In the Corporation Letter Book of that year[1] the 'Maunciple of Lyncolnesynne' is mentioned. Odgers, however, thought that the reference was to the lawyers in the Bishop of Chichester's Inn,[2] and in truth it might be to either.

The next known reference to the Abbot's property is in the will of Roger Lardener, dated 20 January 1428/9. He bequeathed 'his term of years to come in an inn or tenement set in Holbourne farmed to me by the Abbot of Malmesbury'. Williams thought that this would probably be only 'the brewery attached to Lincoln's Inn'.[3] In any case the name of the Inn is not mentioned in that will. And then, unfortunately, there is a gap until 1525. On 6 February 1525/6[4] the Convent leased to Thomas Dalton for fifty years its lands and tenements, inns, houses etc., gardens etc. belonging to it in the parish of St Andrew in Holborn. The rent was £4, payable to the convent 'or to the Warden of the Chapel of the Holy Virgin in the Monastery aforesaid'. The lease provided that it should be lawful for the convent and the Warden of the Chapel

and all others co-monks of the said monastery to enjoy and use the principal houses in the principal Inn there late called Berealey and now called Castell Alley, to wit, the Hall . . . the Chapel and four chambers in front of it, the kitchen and stabling for their horses . . . in the little garden next the said Inn adjoining and pasture growing in the same, with liberty

[1] W.D. no. 1080.   [2] *Post*, p. 56.   [3] See W.D. no. 1156.
[4] W.D. no. 1157.

to walk in the great garden there at their will as often as they should happen
to come to the city of London or for any occasion of the monastery.

The lessee was to rebuild one brewhouse. The lease became vested
in Henry Willoughby, who purchased the reversion after the dis-
solution of the monastery.

There seems to be no doubt that the Abbot's Inn had dropped the
name of Lincoln's Inn long before 1525, though the monastery still
retained the property at that date. When or why this happened can
only be a matter of conjecture. It might have been not long after the
rent roll assumed its final form, and the most critical period for the
purposes of this Discourse is between 1399, when the Abbot's Inn
still certainly retained the name, and 1422, when the Black Books
open. Did it happen during that period? There are three entries in
the Black Books which may supply the clue.

In 1438 John Row delivered to John Fortescu and others in the
name of the Society to be paid to (blank) Halssewylle for 'the farm of
Lyncollsyn' in arrear for the fifteenth year of Henry VI (1436–7)
in the time of Bartholemew Bolney, then Pensioner, in full payment
40s., out of moneys received by him.[1] Again, in 1442 the Governors
'delivered out of the Treasury two writings obligatory, containing
20 marks, made by W. Taverner, a Fellow of the Society for the
security of two acquittances for the farm of Lincoln's Inn in the
19th and 20th years of Henry VI, which two acquittances were received by the said Governors and remain in the Treasury'.[2] Finally,
in 1456 Robert Folbery was examined in the presence of the Society
touching 40s. which was required of him for the time when he was
Pensioner, which he had retained in his hands, and which he ought
to have paid to Master Thomas Hanwell 'for the farm of Lincoln's
Inn'.[3] Nothing is known of Halswil, or Hanwell, and the farm has
never been identified. The intriguing question is whether there were
transactions between the Society of lawyers in the Bishop's Inn and
the convent, under which the Society became tenants of the farm of
Lincoln's Inn (which may have incorporated the ruined Serjeant's
Inn) and so acquired the use, or the exclusive use, of the name,
while the convent let the Inn which had been described as newly
built in 1380 under another name—(perhaps Berealey or Castell
Alley).[4] If there were any such dealings, they are unlikely to have
occurred after 1422, because there is no hint of them in the Black

---

[1] B.B. I. 8.   [2] *Ibid.* 12.   [3] *Ibid.* 29.   [4] See W.D. nos. 1158, 1159.

Books, and as early as 1438 the Society's relationship to the 'farm of Lincoln's Inn' is treated as a matter of course.

So ends the story of the Abbot's Inn. The theories to which it has given rise must now be discussed.

Turner himself took a very modest view of his discoveries. In the *Athenaeum* of 22 September 1906[1] he wrote:

Thomas of Lincoln may on selling his Inn to the Abbot of Malmesbury have taken up his residence at the Lincoln's Inn of today, which then belonged to the Bishop of Chichester, bringing there a body of apprentices who had lived with him in his old Inn. . . I am not suggesting that this is more than a possible explanation. For my part I am inclined to think that the old view that Lincoln's Inn was once the residence of the Earls of Lincoln whose arms it used is still entitled to respect.

Williams, who so industriously compiled most of the evidence relating to the Inn which Turner had rediscovered, propounded the following theory of the origin of the Society:[2]

The Society of Lincoln's Inn . . . in 1422 . . . was no new society; it had migrated from elsewhere, carrying with it its former name. But there is at present not the slightest evidence that it had been connected in any way with the Inn of the Earl of Lincoln in Shoe Lane. On the contrary it is not improbable that it came from Holborn, where it would have occupied land with a block of houses, a great garden, a hall and a chapel dedicated to St. Mary,[3] lying between Staple Inn on the west, Barnard's Inn on the east, the main road of Holborn on the north, and the Chancellor's ditch on the south. . . After their migration[4] they changed the name of the chapel of St Richard in the Bishop of Chichester's Inn to that of St Mary, to whom their former chapel had been dedicated. But when Richard Kingsmill, who purchased the Inn on behalf of the Benchers in 1580, applied to the Heralds' College for a coat of arms,[5] he obtained for the Society the following. . . As for the canton (being the arms of the Earl), it is only natural that the Society should have sought to perpetuate an honourable tradition. Having a profound veneration for the famous lawyer-administrator, and being in constant remembrance of him by their name, they claimed him as their patron, and were proud to incorporate his arms with their own. Yet Thomas de Lincoln after whom it appears their Society was most probably named, who had been forgotten, is also worthy of recognition in having laid so well the foundation of so durable a structure.

[1] P. 335.   [2] *Op. cit.* section 33.
[3] This chapel was at Malmesbury, and not in Holborn. *Ante*, p. 49.
[4] *Op. cit.* section 35.
[5] The Society had used the arms of Henry de Lacy long before 1580.

But although Williams adopted the view that the Society was probably founded by the Serjeant, and probably migrated from his Inn to the Bishop's Inn, he proceeds upon the hypothesis that it found there on arrival a body of lawyers who may have been established there long before 1338.

Granting them, [he wrote,][1] that a settlement of law students existed at the Bishop's Inn, say, from the time of Ralph de Neville, the great Chancellor, the origin of Lincoln's Inn as an Inn of Court is explained, without any reference to Henry de Lacy. The Society of Lincoln's Inn, coming from Holborn in the year 1422 came to what was already an Inn of Court, with a settlement of students who had congregated there under the previous Chancellors, with chambers, a hall and a chapel in existence before the great Earl of Lincoln's birth, and with Chancery Clerks and Apprentices of the Courts whose predecessors had anciently regarded the Middle Temple as their Alma mater... Under the circumstances, it seems admissible that the Inn was one for the legal profession long before 1338... in 1338 it became discontinued from the Temple; in 1422 it imported another Society from elsewhere and adopted its name.

This reasoning seems to be open to serious criticism. If it is admissible to believe that the Bishop's Inn was occupied (even in part and even subject to reservations) by lawyers 'long before 1338', their Society was certainly not founded by Thomas de Lincoln. On the other hand, that assumption removes the main obstacle to acceptance of the ancient tradition that a society founded by the Earl was brought there by him. There seems to be no ground for associating the foundation of a Society of lawyers with Chancellor Ralph de Neville. If an ancient Society (whether founded by the Earl, or the Chancellor or any other founder except Thomas de Lincoln) was in occupation of part of the Bishop's Inn, but was not called Lincoln's Inn before 1417, it had presumably by then become known by some other name (and of this there is no trace), and if (as the theory presupposes) it had not been founded by the Serjeant, there seems to be no reason why it should have abandoned its own name because other lawyers joined it on a migration from his Inn, unless he was so distinguished that they wanted to adopt him as a second founder. But if their purpose between 1417 and 1422 was to honour themselves by honouring him, his very existence could hardly have been forgotten (as in fact it had been) some fifty years afterwards. Moreover, there is no reason to believe that any body of

[1] *Op. cit.* section 38.

lawyers remained in the Serjeant's Inn after he sold it to the Abbot, though it is not impossible.

There are more probable explanations of the recent discoveries, but these must be reserved for a final chapter.

Williams' theory might have been different and more acceptable if he had been able to suggest a much earlier migration. But he was driven to postulate a migration as late as 1417 because on evidence which he accepted, but which was unknown to Turner, Thomas de Lincoln's property did not lose the name of Lincoln's Inn before that date.

But it is to Odgers and Holdsworth, rather than to Turner or even Williams, that the recent promotion of Thomas de Lincoln to the rank of founder is due. It is now therefore necessary to analyse the material upon which Odgers built the theory which Holdsworth accepted.

Dr Blake Odgers, in his sketch of the history of the four Inns of Court published in *Essays in Legal History* (1913), had not the assistance to be derived from the Abbot's letter,[1] and accordingly he fell into the error of thinking that there was only one Inn upon the property, whereas there were certainly two. Moreover, he seems to have read the symbol in the additional note between *hospitium armigeri* and *magnum hospitium* as *jam*, which it certainly is not. On this double error he built his theory. He argued that between 1399 and the date of the later addition to the rent roll the rent of the Inn had been reduced from £8 to £2 a year because 'the big mansion' had become ruinous now (*jam*), i.e. when the note was added. But it is clear that £8 per annum was the rent of the Abbot's Inn which was built between 1369 and 1380, and that £2 per annum was the rent of the Serjeant's Inn, which had become ruinous. Therefore Odgers seems to have been building upon sand. But he built with assurance.

Hence, [he wrote,] early in the fifteenth century, we find the Society of Lincoln's Inn located in a mansion on the east side of Chancery Lane which had become ruinous. The landlord apparently did nothing towards the repair of the mansion. And so it seems clear that the Society moved across Chancery Lane and entered into occupation of the house and premises of the Bishop of Chichester, which had lain empty since 1412. [There is no evidence of this.] The exact date of this removal we cannot fix, but it must have been before 1422; for in that year commence

[1] *Ante*, p. 46.

the Black Books, the first volume of which is entitled 'Liber Hospitii de Lincolnsin.' (The earliest entries) in this volume show that the persons then in possession of those premises formed a fully established Society, possessing the constitution, powers and privileges of an Inn of Court. And those persons retained their former title of the Society of Lincoln's Inn, and never called themselves Bishop's Inn or Chichester Inn as would have been the case with a society newly created. That the Society of Lincoln's Inn existed before 1422 is clear from the fact that in the Corporation Letter Books one Thomas Brown is described as Maunciple of Lincoln's Inn under date of 1417.

Williams, as has been noted, accepted this as a reference to the Abbot's Lincoln's Inn. It might indeed refer to either. But there is of course no doubt that the Honourable Society existed before 1422. Odgers then refers to the payment of rent for 'the farm of Lincoln's Inn' in 1438 and concludes:

that is to say, the Society of Lincoln's Inn, now settled in the Bishop of Chichester's mansion, was still paying the identical rent of 40/– which it paid at the commencement of the century for the ruinous hospitium of Lyncolnesynne.[1]

Then under the sub-title *The Legend of the Earl of Lincoln*, he continues:

But as time ran on, the King's serjeant was forgotten; no one remembered Thomas de Lincoln and his hospice to the north of the Chancellor's ditch, and men began to wonder why the Society was called Lincoln's Inn. The name did not seem to have any connexion with the history of the Society's present abode; from what source did it come? And someone must have recollected that there was a famous man in the reign of Edward I, and who resided somewhere in the locality; possibly he was the founder of the Society. And in that uncritical age the suggestion soon found favour.[2] [And later:] there is not the faintest evidence that any professors or students of the law ever occupied any portion of Earl de Lacy's house or grounds.[3]

But all this reasoning ultimately depends upon an erroneous identification of the Abbot's new Inn with the Serjeant's Inn which was in a state of ruin.

Holdsworth, in the third edition of his *History of English Law* (1923), adopted the argument of Odgers as probably correct, apparently without independent inquiry, as appears from the following passage:

[1] Pp. 252–3.   [2] Pp. 253–4.   [3] P. 255.

Mr Turner[1] and Dr. Blake Odgers[2] have suggested another theory, which is probably correct. It appears that in the middle of the fourteenth century there was a King's Serjeant named Thomas de Lincoln, who owned a piece of property on the site of the present Furnival Street. This property was the earliest house of the Society of Lincoln's Inn. By three deeds of 1364, 1366 and 1369 the fee simple of this property was conveyed by Thomas de Lincoln to the Abbot of Malmesbury. He let it to the Society at a rent of £8; but a little later the rent was reduced to £4 on account of its ruinous condition. It was probably on account of the ruinous condition of the property that the Society moved into the house of the Bishop of Chichester. The date at which the removal took place was between 1412 and 1422. Till the former date the Bishop was living in the house. At the latter date the Black Books show that the Society was in occupation. Thomas de Lincoln, the King's Serjeant, having been forgotten, the name was accounted for by a wholly imaginary connection of the Society with Henry de Lacy, Earl of Lincoln.[3]

This reasoning must, however, be rejected upon the same grounds upon which Odgers' theory had to be rejected. It is based upon the same double error. But the problems created by the discovery of the Abbot's Lincoln's Inn cannot be so easily disposed of, and must be further considered in the concluding chapter.

[1] *The Athenaeum*, 22 September 1906, p. 334.
[2] *Essays in Legal History*, 1913, pp. 250–5.
[3] *A History of English Law*, 3rd. edn. 1923, II, p. 500.

CHAPTER V

THE EARL OF LINCOLN

THE two positive results of recent research seem to have been to disprove Baildon's theory of a migration from Furnival's Inn, and to discredit attempts to depose Henry de Lacy in favour of Thomas de Lincoln. We must now turn to the Earl of Lincoln himself.

Sulyard unreservedly attributes to him a dominant role in the establishment of the Inns of Court. He describes him as Lord High Steward, and as in sole charge of the administration of justice under the King, and he states that it was through his wise policy that companies gathered together in places of residence to study law.[1] In another passage he writes:

The said Earl Lacy lies honourably entombed in our Lady Chapel in 'Powles'[2] whereunto he was in his lifetime a noble benefactor and . . . there is to be seen cut out in stone upon his tomb the proportions of mourners in the habits . . . of serjeants-at-law with their coifs and hoods, gripping in one hand a pair of gloves, which coifs, hoods gloves are (as they then were) the very proper signals of . . . belonging to a serjeant-at-law being first raised to that dignity.[3]

These passages raise three novel questions. The first—and it is an unexpected question to which an unexpected answer must be given —is whether the Earl was ever Lord High Steward, or more accurately Steward of England. The second question—also surprising and likewise requiring a surprising answer—is whether sole charge of the administration of justice under the King ever appertained to that office. The third question, which is more important and should not be unexpected, is whether the Earl, even if never Steward, was responsible for the policy which led to the foundation of the Inns of Court generally, and in particular Lincoln's Inn. Before attempting to answer any of these questions, it is necessary to take into account some of the known aspects of the Earl's distinguished career, and then to review briefly the history of the stewards and their powers, actual or imagined. This indeed may again cause surprise, because lists of stewards have been prepared by more than

---

[1] *Ante*, p. 38.   [2] The old St Paul's, destroyed in the Great Fire.
[3] Fo. 3.

one writer, and the Earl's name is not among them. But closer inspection discloses a gap which he would neatly fill. Again, history would be expected to give a clear answer to the question whether the office carried with it such exalted powers over the administration of justice; and so it does—an emphatic negative. But many writers in the seventeenth century concur in assigning these imaginary powers to the hereditary steward, and this historical fiction can in their case be traced to a single document. Moreover, this allegation by Sulyard seems to have its origin either in the same document or in one that preceded it. Therefore the accuracy of Sulyard's claim appears to be bound up with the historical value of that tract. Here, again, the surprising result of inquiry will be that the tract, never yet satisfactorily explained, would accord with a theory which would support Sulyard's proposition, if confined to the Earl of Lincoln. But there is no evidence to support this theory, and perhaps a less interesting explanation may have to be preferred.

The narrative which now follows recalls only those episodes in the life of the Earl which are relevant to the discussion of these problems. It is necessary to do this because although the Earl has always been regarded as a great soldier and administrator and as a close friend of Edward I, no writer has hitherto stressed the dominant role which Sulyard claims for him in the administration of law and the training of lawyers. For example, J. E. Bailey in his Introduction to 'Two *Compoti*' (Accounts) of the Earl's Stewards[1] describes him as 'one of the most conspicuous and powerful barons of the realm', and records that numerous writs of summons for his attendance at Parliament were addressed to him from 1276 to 1309, that he was also summoned to the King's Councils, and was a close friend of the King. But he does not make any specific reference to his work in the field of law. In this respect he follows the early chroniclers, who recount his exploits in war and diplomacy, but with only one important exception, give no hint of his legal activities. Yet this exception may supply the clue.

After discussing the King's place in history as a lawgiver, Holdsworth wrote: 'if the comprehensive character of Edward I's legislation entitles him, as Lambard thought,[2] to be accounted our English Justinian, Robert Burnell has some claim to be called our English Tribonian'.[3] Burnell, Bishop of Bath and Wells, was Chancellor of

---

[1] Published by the Chetham Society in 1884, pp. v, vii.   [2] *Archeion*, p. 67.
[3] *History of English Law*, II. 292. This is a reference to the *Prooemium* (Preface)

England from 1274 until his death. But he died in 1292. Both he
and the Earl of Lincoln had gone to France with the King in 1286.
'On Edward's return to England in 1289', wrote Horwood, 'after
three years' absence, he found that the clamour against his judges
was great by reason of their injustice, extortion and corruption . . .
so after due inquiry, the blow fell, the next year being in the words
of Walsingham . . . *Justiciariis exitialis*.'[1] Commissioners were appointed to inquire into these matters—'*ad recipiendam querelam de
injuriis per ministros suos, dum fuit trans mare, populo communi
illatis*'.[2] Burnell presided, but the Earl of Lincoln was also one of the
Commissioners. It is unnecessary to enlarge upon what Maitland
called 'our one great judicial scandal'[3] beyond mentioning that the
report of the Commission in 1290 was followed by a wholesale
removal of justices. More relevant for the present purpose is
Holdsworth's comment upon it: 'the whole episode helped in
no slight degree to forward the success of Edward's legislative re-
forms'.[4]

Burnell died suddenly and was buried at Wells on 23 November
1292. As has been stated before,[5] there is no record of the steps taken
by John de Metingham or his fellow judges to carry out the Order
de attornatis et apprenticiis made in that year. The Earl of Lincoln,
who had been one of the Commissioners in 1289, and has been described by Stubbs as the King's closest counsellor,[6] may well have
played an important part. But first of all it will be convenient to complete the known story of the Earl's life.

In 1292 he was at Berwick during deliberations about the Scottish
succession, and in the same year he was appointed to decide on the
claims of William de Ros and John de Vaux. In 1293 he was on an
embassy to France, and from 1294 until the spring of 1295 he was
involved in military operations in Wales. Edmund Earl of Lancaster,

---

to the first book of the Institutes of the Emperor Justinian which contains the
following passage (translated): 'then we extended our care to the vast volumes of
old jurisprudence, and we have now fulfilled our desperate undertaking by grace
from heaven, like voyagers over the deep. And when this had been completed with
the providence of God, we summoned Tribonian, a person of distinction, a master
and former quaestor of our sacred palace, and also Theophilus and Dorotheus . . .
and entrusted them with the task of composing a book of Institutes by our authority and under our guidance'.

[1] *Year Books of the reign of K. Edw. I.* Years 20/21, ed. Horwood, 1866.
[2] *Annales Londinienses*, ed. Stubbs, 1882.
[3] Quoted by Holdsworth, *History of English Law*, 3rd edn. II. 295.
[4] *Ibid.* II. 299.   [5] *Ante*, p. 35.   [6] *Constitutional History*, 1906, II. 333.

Steward of England, died in 1296.[1] In 1298 the Earl of Lincoln, described as *consanguineus* to the King,[2] was appointed to arrange a marriage between Edward, Prince of Wales, and Isabella of France. In 1299 he attended a Council at York to deliberate upon the affairs of Scotland, where he campaigned in the following year. Later in 1300 he was on missions to the Pope and to France. In 1301 he visited Scotland. Between 1302 and 1304 he took part in negotiations with France, visiting there in 1304. In September 1305 he was a member of a Commission to arrange the affairs of Scotland, and in October he was sent on another mission to the Pope. He was again described as *consanguineus*.[3] On his return he was publicly received in London.

Eodem anno (1306) die sancti Matthaei apostoli, comes Lincolniae venit Londinias de Lugduno cum sociis, majore et pluribus aliis de villa Londiniana sibi abstantibus.[4]

He returned from Lyons with his associates, the Mayor and most of the citizens of the town of London meeting him in the way.

In the same year he performed a ceremonial office which may be significant:

Eodem anno, xi° Kalendas Junii qui dicitur dies Pentecostes Edwardus princeps Walliae factus fuit miles apud Westmonasterium a domino Edwardo rege patre suo; comites Lyncolniae et Herefordiae calcaria pedibus praedicti principis apposuerunt.[5]

Edward, Prince of Wales, was knighted at Westminster by his father the King; the Earls of Lincoln and Hereford put spurs upon his feet.

At this time de Lacy was at the zenith of his power. It is recorded in the Chronicle of Lanercost:

interim autem rex Angliae, collecto exercitu, misit dominum Edwardum filium suum supradictum, quem tunc fecerat militem Londiniis cum aliis trecenis secum, et comitem Lincolniae cujus consilio omnia faceret dictus dominus Edwardus, ut persequeretur dictum Robertum de Bruce qui se regem fecerat appelari.[6]

Meanwhile the King of England, having assembled an army, sent Edward his aforesaid son, whom he had then knighted in London, and other

---

[1] The relevance of this date appears later.   [2] Rymer, *Foedera*, I. 905.
[3] *Ibid.* 974.
[4] *Annales Londinienses*, ed. Stubbs. 'Chronicles Edw. I and II', I. 144.
[5] *Annales Londinienses*, I. 146.
[6] The Chronicle of Lanercost (1201–1346) transcribed from the Cottonian MS. by Stevenson, 1839.

three hundred men with him, and the Earl of Lincoln, to whose counsel Edward was told to have regard in all things, in order to pursue the aforesaid Robert Bruce who had made himself to be called king.

In 1307 the Earl of Lincoln was one of the Commissioners appointed to hold a Parliament at Carlisle, and in the Parliament Roll[1] he is named next after the Prince of Wales. He marched with the King to Scotland, and was present at his death.

But his relations with the new King were very different. When he ascended the throne, the Earl, after blessing God for the happy beginning of the new reign, expressed a wish that the King should confirm by writ the promise to ratify whatever the nation should determine[2]—an ominous beginning—and at the coronation, Gaveston carried the crown, and the Earl of Lancaster bore the sword of St Edward called *curtana*. Very soon afterwards, in about February 1307/8, that Earl was appointed Steward of England, and if the Earl of Lincoln ever held that office, his term was at an end. But this need not have brought to a close his efforts to promote legal education, because, in spite of his political difficulties, he was still held in high esteem, and again held high office. His actions during this comparatively short period were 'perhaps due to the conflict between loyalty to his old master's son and his old master's policy'.[3] For it has been said that 'he was Gaveston's chief supporter, but through the latter's ingratitude he came to be the chief of his enemies',[4] and he disliked both the King's favourite and the King's attitude to the people's will. However, he was one of the 'Ordainers' in 1310 and he was actually appointed 'warden' (custos) of England when Edward II set out for Scotland. *Reliquit autem rex, antequam versus Scotiam properasset, dominum Henricum de Lacy comitem Lincolniae custodem Angliae qui commoravit apud Londinias, sed mors, quae inimica est homini, ipsum ab hoc saeculo eripuit . . . sequenti anno* (1311).[5] He died on 5 February 1311, and was buried *cum maximo honore*.[6] *Vir illustris in consilio, strenuus in omni guerra et proelio, Princeps militie in Anglia et in omni regno ornatissimus*, saith the *Booke of Dunmow*.[7]

Such then is the known story of his life, and it contains no reference to the Stewardship of England. Yet if the *M.T.MS.* can be

---

[1] Roll Parl. i. 188/9.　　　　　[2] Stubbs, *Annales Londinienses*, ii. 333.
[3] *Dictionary of National Biography*.　[4] *Annales Londinienses*, ii. 155.
[5] *Ibid.* i. 175.　　[6] *Annales Paulini* in the same volume, p. 269.
[7] Quoted by Weever, *Ancient Funerall Monuments* (1631), p. 365.

relied on, Sulyard related that he was 'Lord High Steward of England'. This indeed sounds like a seventeenth-century title, springing from the legendary history of the office which will soon be discussed. Experience of the *M.T.MS.* shows that the author's quotations are generally reasonably accurate, but often textually inexact. He therefore may have added the words 'Lord High'; on the other hand, the legend of their exalted powers may have been well under way even in Sulyard's time. However this may be, the true question must be whether the Earl filled a gap in the hereditary sequence of the Stewards of England. The authentic history of these Stewards was for the first time carefully recorded by Harcourt in his book, *His Grace the Steward and Trial by Peers*.[1] The term 'Steward' (*Senescallus*) came into general use on the accession of Richard I (1189). The privilege conferred by this hereditary office in the Royal Household was that of 'serving at the royal table, with perhaps the additional right of carrying a sword at the Coronations'. When Richard I was crowned, there were two stewards. The Earl of Leicester carried a sword at the ceremony. The other steward was the Earl of Norfolk. There was a dispute between these two Earls on the accession of King John, as a result of which the Earl of Norfolk withdrew for valuable consideration. In 1206 the fourth Simon de Montfort succeeded to the earldom of Leicester and the hereditary office of steward.[2] The fifth Simon de Montfort was legally appointed to the office in 1238–9, though he had already served as steward on 20 January 1236 when Eleanor, consort of Henry III, was crowned, and Harcourt considered that he raised the office to a position of considerable importance on the foundation of his own achievements.[3]

It was he who first assumed the title of 'Steward of England' (*Senescallus Angliae*) in pursuance of, wrote Harcourt, 'a deliberate policy of self-aggrandisement', and the stewardship was then 'in course of becoming the first great office of state', but 'it fell into weak hands'.[4] For with the battle of Evesham came the end of the power of the de Montforts, and Edmund, younger son of Henry III, became possessed of the earldom and stewardship in 1275, but the office was conferred on him for his own life alone.[5]

This is the genesis of the gap, and it is therefore desirable to refer

---

[1] Longmans, Green and Co. (1907).
[2] Harcourt, *His Grace the Steward and Trial by Peers*, pp. 72, 74, 76.
[3] *Ibid.* pp. 84, 86.   [4] *Ibid.* pp. 122, 128.   [5] *Ibid.* p. 139.

to the actual grant by Edward I, as recorded in Patent Roll 3 Edw. I.[1]

Pro Edmundo fratre regis—Rex omnibus etc. salutem:
Sciatis quod de gratia nostra speciali concessimus pro nobis et hereditibus nostris Edmundo fratri karissimo senescalciam Anglie cum omnibus ad eandem senescalciam pertinentibus quam Simon de Montforti quondam comes Leycestrie aliquando habuit habendum et tenendum eidem Edmundo *quoad vixerit*.

For Edmund brother of the King—The King to all etc. Greeting:
Know ye that of our special grace we have granted for ourselves and our heirs to Edmund our most dear brother the stewardship of England with all that appertains to the same stewardship which Simon de Montfort, formerly Earl of Leicester at one time held, to have and to hold to the same Edmund so long as he shall have lived.

Harcourt records that he was not a man of great parts. 'We hear nothing of the stewardship during this period; it simply relapsed into obscurity.'[2] He died (having been created Earl of Lancaster) on 5 June 1296.

Of this period (not long after the crucial date of the Order in Council of 1292) Harcourt wrote as follows:

The stewardship once more became extinct. Edmund's son Thomas succeeded to the titles and estates. On the 7th of July 1307, Edward the First died at Burgh-on-Sands by Solway Water, and the Prince of Wales came to the throne. At this King's coronation (February 25th, 1307/8) the Gascon favourite Gaveston took the chief place in the pageant and carried the crown; but the Earl of Lancaster bore the sword 'Curtana' (the sword of St. Edward) a circumstance to be noted, and it is fairly probable that he claimed and was allowed to act as steward at the feast in Westminster Hall. At all events, shortly after the coronation, Edward the Second by letters patent conferred the stewardship of England on Thomas and his heirs in tail, as being an office appurtenant, so it was said, to the earldom of Leicester.[3]

Obviously there was room for a stewardship between 1296 and 1307. There may well have been some dispute, and a claim to revive the hereditary succession of the Earls of Leicester when Edward II came to the throne. But whether or not that was so, the existence of the gap seems to have been proved.

Thomas of Lancaster was in due course beheaded. On the accession of Edward III, his brother Henry became Earl of Lancaster,

---

[1] Membrane 30, quoted by Harcourt, *ibid.* p. 163.   [2] *Ibid.* pp. 139, 140.
[3] *Ibid.* pp. 141–2.

and he seems to have established his claim to the stewardship about 1330; he died in 1345.[1] He was succeeded as steward by his son Henry (afterwards created Duke of Lancaster) who died in 1360/1.[2] John of Gaunt was created Duke of Lancaster in 1362, and about the same time he was recognized as Earl of Leicester and Steward of England.[3] On the death of Edward III, he assumed control of the preparations for crowning Richard II, and set the precedent of a 'Court of Claims'.[4] For himself he claimed the office of steward as Earl of Leicester, the right to carry the sword *curtana* as Duke of Lancaster, and the right of carving before the King as Earl of Lincoln. All these claims were allowed.[5] He died in 1398/9.[6] On or before 4 October 1399 Henry IV appointed Thomas Plantagenet (afterwards the Duke of Clarence) Steward of England.[7] He fell at the battle of Beaugé, and after his death the stewardship was never regranted except for particular occasions.[8] This was the position when Sulyard wrote between 1514 and 1540.

When the *M.T.MS.* was compiled early in the seventeenth century, the court of the Lord High Steward had become established. Harcourt regards the case of the Earl of Warwick in 1499 as the first genuine case in that court,[9] and on that occasion the King appointed the Earl of Oxford to be 'Lord High Steward of England' for the trial.[10] The history of that court has no connection with Sulyard or the Earl of Lincoln, but it may explain why the author of the *M.T.MS.* used that phrase when quoting from Sulyard's manuscript.

At the beginning of the seventeenth century the Society of Antiquaries took a lively interest in the antiquity, authority and succession of the High Stewards of England. It was the theme of a group of discourses, which were printed in the enlarged (1771) edition of Hearne's *Curious Discourses*. Most of them seem to have been read before the Society. The first of the set was composed by Sir Robert Cotton (1571–1631) who made the famous collection of manuscripts now in the British Museum, and among them are three copies of the tract which has long bedevilled the history of stewards. Others were by Townsend (1603), Holland (1603), Thynne, Tate (1603), Davys, Camden, Agarde and two anonymous authors. Their contents are startling. Cotton for instance wrote:

the two principall species or kinds are the grand regall office of high

[1] P. 172. [2] P. 173. [3] P. 176. [4] Pp. 176–7. [5] Pp. 182–3.
[6] P. 187. [7] P. 189. [8] P. 191. [9] P. 429. [10] P. 431.

F

steward of England, and the oeconomicall office of steward of the King's household. The one being a chiefe officer over the whole state . . . immediately and universally representing the power and person of the king . . . the jurisdiction of the first surmounting the greatest peers.[1]

Again Townsend wrote:

The office since the conquest hath long continued by descent inheritably in the family of the ancient earls of Leicester, and so remained until it was transferred to the house of Lancaster after the death of Simon de Montfort.[2]

Sir Edward Coke wrote in the fourth part of his Institutes, posthumously published in 1648:[3]

And in respect his power before it was limited was so transcendent, I finde no mention made of this great Officer in any of our ancient authors, the Mirror, Bracton, Britton or Fleta. It seemeth they liked not to treat of his authority. Neither do I finde him in any Act of Parliament nor in any book case before 1 H.4 and very few since.

Doubtless Cotton's assertion of the superior powers of the Steward rests upon the tract which he preserved. The tract is intituled *Hic annotatur quis sit seneschallus Angliae et quid ejus officium* (a note on the steward of England and his office). The first two sentences read as follows:

Senescalacia Anglie pertinet ad comitivam Leycestrie et pertinuit ab antiquo.
Et sciendum quod ejus officium est supervidere et regulare sub rege et immediate post regem totum regnum Anglie et omnes ministros legum infra idem regnum temporibus pacum et guerrarum in forma que subsequitur.

The stewardship of England appertains to the earl of Leicester and has appertained from of old.
And know ye that his office is to supervise and regulate under the king and immediately after the king the whole realm of England and all officers of the law within the same realm in times of peace and war in manner following.

The tract is too long to be set out here in full:[4] but it may be said that the earlier part seems to relate exclusively to abuses in the administration of justice by judicial officers which caused suffering to

---

[1] Vol. II, p. 2.   [2] *Ibid* p. 15.   [3] P. 59.
[4] It is printed in full by Harcourt (*op. cit.* p. 164) and translated on p. 148.

litigants. It begins by seeking to enable members of the public to petition the King in Parliament through the intervention of the Steward to redress abuses in any court and to call the highest judicial officers to account, including the Chancellor of England himself, the justices, treasurers, barons and chamberlains of the Exchequer. It refers to judicial corruption and ambiguities in the law. If the law was doubtful, 'the Chancellor and such like officer' was to be excused, and Parliament was to clarify the law. But if the law was clear, and delays and defaults in processes and judgments were due to judicial misconduct or ignorance the judges were to be admonished or removed.

So far the tract seems singularly appropriate to the judicial scandals which Edward I found on his return from France, and is just such a mandate for reform as he might have given to his closest counsellor if he was to supervise and regulate the administration of justice with authority over all judges except the King himself. But suddenly, with the word 'likewise', the document introduces an entirely new theme—the relation between the king and his 'evil counsellors'. 'Likewise it is the Steward's office (to intervene) if the King have evil counsellors about him who advise him to do such things as are plainly and publicly to his dishonour or disherison, and to the public hurt and destruction of his people' and from there to the end the tract is altogether political and appropriate to the reign of Edward II, ending with the fall and beheading of Peter Gaveston.

This tract has long been a historical puzzle. Tate, in his *Discourse*,[1] wrote in 1603 'I am very suspicious, for the examples added to confirm the theorick thereof by practice, the historyes disprove. And if he be made supervisor and rector sub rege, and immediate post regem totius regni, what place is left for the chiefe justice of England?' A dissertation attributed to S. N. Russell on 'The Lord High Steward of England' (1776) in *Hill's Law Tracts* observes: 'It cannot but surprise the reader to see an office of so much pretension, so little understood and so rarely exercised, during a course of 300 years' and adds in reference to the tract, 'it is very certain that the author of that record mistook the Justiciar of England for the hereditary Seneschal'. He chided Sir Edward Coke for his credulity.[2]

Harcourt treats the document as having been produced in its entirety after the fall of Gaveston, and explains it by drawing a parallel

[1] *Op. cit.* p. 32.   [2] Pp. 70, 133.

between Edward II and Henry III—both foolish and extravagant with a predilection for unpopular foreigners. In both cases the hereditary steward led the opposition—in one case Simon de Montfort and in the other Thomas Earl of Lancaster. 'Concisely stated,' he wrote,[1] 'the position of affairs was this: the people had various specific constitutional grievances which they desired to have redressed; the barons had their own personal grievances, and were exasperated by the offensive behaviour of Gaveston.' Harcourt added:[2] 'This particular document clearly forms the root of title to the jurisdiction conferred on, or assumed by, the steward of England in the reign of Richard the Second. Eventually this dignitary acquired settled functions very different from those claimed by Thomas, but only by a modification, gradual and easily traced, of the prerogatives asserted in the tract.'

It seems to be reasonably clear that Sulyard either had access to this tract, or had access to an earlier document which embodied the first part of it. The similarity of language is too close to be accidental. But the question to be solved is whether it was the tract itself, or an earlier document. If it was the tract itself, then Sulyard made a curious double mistake. He must have mistaken the Earl of Leicester for the Earl of Lincoln, and he must also have overlooked the primary allegation of the document that the office had always been hereditary. It is true that Sulyard is unique in asserting that Lincoln was Steward; but all writers except Harcourt have overlooked the gap which undoubtedly occurred; and it is just as likely to have been filled by Lincoln as left vacant. Indeed, it is just the office which he might have been expected to have filled. He was not only the King's closest counsellor; he was very close to the throne, and some of the ceremonial duties which he is known to have discharged would well befit a high steward. Moreover, he was constantly employed to deal on behalf of the King with legal and constitutional questions, and in particular, as one of the Commissioners, to deal with the judicial scandals which were found to be rife on the King's return from France in 1289. The first part of the tract (and the dichotomy is very evident) would be just such a mandate as the King might have given him in the circumstances; he would have thus been the King's representative for reform. Nor would the combination of the stewardship and legal reform sound unnatural to a generation which remembered how Simon de Montfort climbed up-

[1] P. 143.   [2] P. 151.

wards on the ladder of this office, and was familiar with similar developments on the Continent. No satisfactory explanation of the tract has yet been given. In its present form it looks like political propaganda on behalf of an Earl of Leicester, and the second half would be appropriate to the troubles of Edward II. But the first part does not fit that reign at all. No doubt it is strange that there is nowhere any other record of the Earl of Lincoln having filled the gap. But the history of that period is somewhat fragmentary, and the claimants for an otherwise hereditary office had every reason to conceal the gap.

However this may be, it would be wrong to assert as a fact that the Earl of Lincoln was Steward of England, or that, if he was, he was given by means of a constitutional fiction such exceptional and overriding powers for the specific purpose of legal reform on his appointment. It is not inherently improbable. But such a proposition could not safely be accepted upon the uncorroborated testimony of a single writer when chances of error are in such abundant supply. Had it been capable of acceptance, it would of course have supplied the coping-stone to Sulyard's theory of the origins of the Inns of Court. But as it is, his theory, if valid, must be proved by other evidence; and such evidence seems to be forthcoming.

During the period in which the vital Order in Council was made, the Earl was summoned to the King's Councils,[1] and his must have been a powerful voice there. He had been with the King in France, and had returned with him to face judicial abuses. The King turned for assistance, not only to Burnell, his Chancellor, but also to Lincoln, since both were among the Commissioners who were appointed to deal with this crisis in legal administration.[2] And it was this crisis which paved the way for legal reform.[3] It is hardly possible to doubt that Burnell and Lincoln advised the King to promulgate the Order in Council and undertook to put it into operation. When Burnell died in the same year (1292), and therefore before the Order can have been carried out, it is very reasonable to suppose that Henry de Lacy took his place (to borrow Holdsworth's phrase) as the King's 'Tribonian'. It is true that there is no actual record of this, except in the narrative of Sulyard. But then, as Dugdale and Pollock have pointed out, there is no record anywhere of the manner in which the judges carried out the Order. But they certainly did so, and it is hardly possible that they failed to take advice from the

[1] *Ante*, p. 59.   [2] *Ante*, p. 60.   [3] *Ante*, p. 60.

Earl, who was growing in the meantime even greater in stature. In the year in which the Order was promulgated, he took part in deliberations upon the Scottish succession, and he was appointed to adjudicate upon the claims of William de Ros and John de Vaux.[1] In 1299 and again in 1305 he took part in deliberations in Council upon Scottish affairs,[1] and in 1306 he was given a civic welcome in London.[1] In the following year he was named next after the Prince of Wales on the Roll of Parliament.[2] And, although when Edward II came to the throne, he was no longer the King's closest counsellor, his power and popularity suffered no notable decline. Can there be any doubt upon this record that part at least of his popularity must have been due to his devotion to justice for the people, as manifested to them in particular by his zeal for legal reform? And in the end, the record in stone upon his tomb may be better evidence of his work for the law than the witness of an ancient chronicler might have been. It is difficult otherwise to see what he had to do with serjeants-at-law, so that they should have been chosen as his principal mourners.

'The said Earl Lacy', wrote Sulyard, 'lies honourably entombed in our Lady Chapel in "Powles". There is to be seen upon his tomb the proportions of mourners in the habits of . . . (laceration) serjeants-at-law with their coifs and hoods, gripping in one hand a pair of gloves.' This tomb was of course destroyed in the Great Fire of 1666, but there is a plate of it by Hollar in the British Museum,[3] described as *tumulus Henrici de Lacie Comitis Lincolniae inter capellas Beatae Mariae et St. Dunstani*, which shows a recumbent figure with head resting on a cushion and a dog at his feet, and along the length of the plinth are ten mourners set in niches under Gothic arches.[4] This plate is reproduced, by permission of the trustees of the British Museum, in this volume.

The evidence of the tomb at the close of such a life as this seems to warrant acceptance of Sulyard's claim that through his wise policy companies were gathered together in places of residence to study law.

---

[1] *Ante*, pp. 60, 61.   [2] *Ante*, p. 62.

[3] No. 2311. See also Dugdale, *St Pauls*, p. 84.

[4] Weever, in *Ancient Funerall Monuments* (1631), described the tomb as follows: 'Henry Lacy, Earle of Lincolne lieth here entombed in the new worke, which was of his owne foundation, under a goodly monument with his armed pourtraiture crosse-legged, as one that had professed his utmost endeavour for defence of the holy land' (p. 365).

CHAPTER VI

ASSESSMENTS AND CONJECTURES

It is impossible to look back upon the earliest recorded accounts of the beginnings of the Inns of Court without noting the contrast between the confident assertions of the manner in which they in general came into being and the guarded statements about the origins of Lincoln's Inn in particular. This contrast is apparent in Sulyard's narrative, the earliest so far known and certainly written before 1540. He attributed the foundation of the Inns to the 'wisdom and policy' of the Earl of Lincoln; but of the ancient tradition of the establishment of Lincoln's Inn, he would say no more than that 'it bears likelihood of truth'.[1] Stow, it is true, attributed the foundation of Lincoln's Inn to the Earl without reservation.[2] But this was certainly because he located the Earl's own Inn on the west side of Chancery Lane which modern research has proved to be mistaken. Dugdale, on the other hand, only accepted this theory with a caution: 'direct proof thereof from good authority, I have not as yet seen any'.[3] If the beginnings of Lincoln's Inn were not remembered with certainty even for 150 years, only a lucky chance (which has not yet happened) could provide real proof now. On the other hand, modern research has done much to reveal probabilities and disprove erroneous theories, and to this work the *M.T.MS.* (which may be provisionally assigned to William Hakewill) has made a notable contribution. Moreover, it has thrown a new and suggestive light upon the less obscure problem of the general origins of the Inns.

To associate them with the conditions prevailing in the time of Edward I, and with his initiative for legal reform and education, as exemplified by the Order in Council of 1292 is no new idea. Indeed, it is now generally accepted doctrine. No better account of those conditions could be devised than that given by Sir Frederick Pollock to the Canadian Guests in 1931, part of which has already been cited.[4] In a later passage he (in common with other writers) associates the movement for 'regular permanent societies, with something like the common life and discipline of a gild, something like the systematic teaching and discussion of a university, and govern-

---

[1] *Ante*, p. 39.   [2] *Ante*, p. 38.   [3] *Ante*, p. 12.   [4] *Ante*, p. 33.

ing bodies of ancients who may present suitable candidates to the king's judges to be approved and licensed as advocates' with that Order in Council.[1] There is nothing therefore novel or surprising in the account of these matters which the author of the *M.T.MS.* himself gives.[2] The new point is in his extract from Sulyard's manuscript, and the emphasis which Sulyard places upon the part played by the Earl of Lincoln. To him Sulyard attributes the movement— to his 'wisdom and policy'. No writer has hitherto assigned to him such a dominant role, although he has always been regarded as an intimate friend of King Edward I and a distinguished soldier and administrator. But Sulyard's testimony cannot be ignored. His is the earliest known record by a legal writer, and there is corroboration in the evidence of the tomb.

Sulyard based the paramount authority with which he clothed the Earl upon a positive assertion that he was Lord High Steward or at any rate, Steward of England. 'Lord High Steward of England to which [saith Mr Sulyard] appertained immediately under the King the sole administration of justice, and to have a due respect unto the execution of the same'.[3] This assertion raises two separate questions: (1) whether the Earl ever held that office at all and (2) whether the office was endowed with such authority. Strangely enough, although there is no evidence that he ever was Steward of England, a gap has been proved between the death of the Earl of Lancaster, who was appointed for life only, in 1296 and the appointment of a successor on a hereditary footing in 1307–8, and no occupant for the gap has ever been named. Indeed the gap itself was only discovered by Harcourt during this century,[4] and of course all hereditary claimants had an interest in concealing the gap. Moreover, although it is certain that in England hereditary stewards had no such exalted powers in the field of law, it was not long before then that Simon de Montfort had attempted to raise the office to a position of political eminence—a circumstance which may well have led Edward I to limit the appointment which he made to a life interest. Furthermore, Sulyard had almost certainly seen a document which claimed such powers for the hereditary steward, and the origin and purpose of the document, or of a later document based upon it, is still an enigma of history. It would not be surprising, therefore, if Edward I did in fact make use of the gap to appoint his viceroy for

[1] *Ante*, p. 34.   [2] *Ante*, p. 37.   [3] Fo. 2d. *Ante*, p. 38.
[4] *Ante*, p. 68.

legal reform to that office, and endow him with the special powers which the earlier part of the document claims for it. Sulyard may, however, have been misled by the document which he saw (though this would have involved a double error), and it certainly gave rise to many misconceptions in the seventeenth century. It would be unsafe therefore to build upon so uncertain a foundation, although his very ancient record cannot be dismissed as inherently improbable.

But it would seem that, whether or not the Earl was ever appointed to the stewardship, there is enough circumstantial evidence to support Sulyard's claim that he played a dominant part in setting up the communities of lawyers, some of which became Inns of Court. His must have been a powerful and respected voice in the King's Council .When the King had to deal with serious abuses in the judicial system, he turned to Burnell and Lincoln, and this crisis paved the way to legal reform. It seems reasonable to assume that they advised him to adopt the course embodied in the Order in Council of 1292, and that he relied on them both to see it carried out. When Burnell died almost immediately, it may be supposed that the Earl took his place for this purpose. There is no record of this elsewhere; but then there is no record of the manner in which the Order in Council was put into operation. There is evidence that the Earl enjoyed popularity as well as power; and much of this may fairly be laid to the credit of his zeal for legal reform. Finally, the principal mourners on his tomb were serjeants-at-law, and no others; and if he had no closer connection with legal administration than is disclosed in the narratives of the chroniclers, it is hard to understand why they alone should have been chosen to weep for a man so eminent in politics and war. These reflections seem to justify Sulyard's claim that through his wise policy companies were gathered together in places of residence to study law.[1]

This conclusion is a double-edged weapon in its relation to the foundation of Lincoln's Inn. On the one hand, Henry de Lacy was just such a legal reformer as might be expected to found an Inn of Court; on the other, he was just such a distinguished legal ancestor as any Inn would have wished to claim, honouring him and honoured by bearing his name, with his permission, or even perhaps without. But these alternatives do coalesce at one point; they give strong support to the view that the Inn, however founded, was

[1] *Ante*, p. 39.

named after him. Indeed if (as seems to be the case for reasons which will shortly appear) Thomas de Lincoln can be disregarded, it is well-nigh proved that the Society bears the name of that great pioneer in the movement for legal education, and of none other.

But for the rest, it is a question where lies the burden of proof. For if the ancient tradition has to be proved, the caution voiced by Sulyard and Dugdale must still be observed. But if it may stand unless disproved, then modern attempts to disprove it seem in their turn to have been disproved by the latest evidence.

Sulyard's narrative does not in terms relate that the place where the Society was established by the Earl was his own Inn. He describes it as very ruinous. 'And the said Earl, as of old time [saith he] by tradition and by the Ancients of this Society is reported, brought a company to this House being at that time very ruinous and out of repair which company [saith he] hath continued the space of 240 years etc. and the company [saith he] was brought hither by the Earl of Lincoln and this House by the said Earl provided for them.'[1] Indeed the proper inference would seem to be that it was not his place of residence, because that would not have been likely to be 'very ruinous and out of repair'. It was apparently Stow who made the mistaken identification of the property in Chancery Lane with the Earl's residence in Shoe Lane, and this of course gave a veneer of certainty to the vague tradition which Sulyard had passed on. Sulyard's version was lost and forgotten; but Stow's lived on to enjoy general acceptance, sometimes however with a caution, until Baildon proved indisputably that this identification was what an equity lawyer calls *falsa demonstratio*.

Baildon, who of course had never heard of Sulyard's version of the ancient tradition, reacted to his own discovery by supposing that the Earl had settled the company of lawyers upon whom he had bestowed his patronage in Thavie's Inn, that they had moved from there to Furnival's Inn, and had later migrated to the Bishop's Inn. But this theory, as manifested in Chapter III, must now be discarded in the light of extracts from the stewards' accounts of that Inn preserved in the *M.T.MS.* which negative the possibility of any considerable exodus from there at the relevant period.

It was no part of the earliest tradition, however, that the premises 'very ruinous and out of repair' which the Earl was said to have provided for the lawyers were an Inn of his or his own place of residence,

[1] Fo. 2d. *Ante*, p. 39. The symbol for *et cetera* appears in the *M.T.MS.* itself.

and, as has already been pointed out,[1] there is no evidence that he ever settled any lawyers in his own Inn in Shoe Lane. It would seem, therefore, that the time has now come to abandon any such ideas, and to revert to Sulyard's older version which, though incapable of corroboration, involves no inherent improbability.

Sulyard related that the Society had continued for the space of 240 years (adding something more that the author of the *M.T.MS.* has most unfortunately left out). This would place its foundation between 1278 and 1300 (the Sulyard manuscript having been written between 1518 and 1540).[2] This would be consistent with foundation by the Earl—any date between 1292 and 1311 would be a likely date—though it would be too early for foundation by the Serjeant—no date before 1331 would be probable in his case.[3]

Now nothing is known about the manner in which the Bishop's palace was used between 1244, when Bishop Neville died there, and 1340; and although it is known that the Bishop had an office or chamber in the Inn in 1340,[4] it is not known whether any Bishop resided there after 1244, or what the state of his London property was at the close of that century, or at the beginning of the next. There is a statement in a 'statute' of the Inn passed in 1466 that Neville's successor Richard de Wyche, who died in 1253, and was afterwards canonized as St Richard of Chichester, was 'late dwelling in this house of Lincoln's Inn';[5] but as Baildon pointed out, this statement 'must be traditional only',[6] and apart from this single reference, he contented himself with the negative proposition that there is no evidence that Neville's successors did *not* reside in the Inn. But it is suggested that this is not enough; and that in the absence of direct evidence, it is just as probable that they did not, at any rate after 1253, except on visits to London for special occasions. There is no doubt that the Bishops had an office or chamber (or perhaps both) in the Inn from 1340 until 1412–13, and they probably had such accommodation from an earlier date, and possibly until a later date. But it is a mistake to infer from this that the Bishops were in *exclusive* occupation of the property, or resided there except at rare intervals for temporary purposes. It seems that Baildon erred in treating such evidence as effectually disposing 'of the statement

[1] *Ante*, p. 42.
[2] *Ante*, p. 11. The MS. describes the gatehouse which was built in 1518, and Sulyard died in 1540.
[3] *Ante*, p. 45. [4] *Ante*, p. 41. [5] B.B. I. 41. [6] B.B. IV. 281.

made by nearly all writers on the subject, to the effect that the
Bishops reserved lodgings for themselves at Lincoln's Inn'.[1] This
was pointed out by Turner, who suggested with good reason that
there might be an element of historical truth in Bishop Montague's
contention in 1635 that 'divers of his predicessors had made leases
to the Benchers of Lincolne's Inne and reserved rent and lodgings
in the Howse when they should repayre to London aboute their
owne busines or his Majesty's affaires'.[2] The Abbot of Malmesbury
made a similar reservation in his charitable assignment of Thomas
de Lincoln's Inn in 1383,[3] and in his lease of the Inn 'late called
Berealey and now called Castell Alley',[4] and there is no reason to
suppose that such an arrangement was uncommon in respect of this
type of property at that period. Bishop Montague was probably in
error when he referred to *leases* to the Benchers. There is no ground
for thinking that the Bishop ever resided in the Inn after 1422, or
that any such reservation was made after that date. Indeed, there are
grounds for thinking that it was not. In 1439 the Bishop appears to
have had a temporary London address in the parish of St Mary
Magdalene in Old Fish Street, in 1444 in the parish of St Mary
Mounthaw, and later at other addresses.[5] Before 1422, on the other
hand, while presumably there must have been some record in
writing of the rent payable, which might well have contained a reservation of the character in question, there is no reason to suppose that
the Society ever had a formal document which would be described
as a lease, or conferred any security of tenure by contract. 'It must
not be forgotten', wrote Baildon,[6]

that during the fourteenth and fifteenth centuries none of the Inns of
Court and Chancery were the owners of their hospitia; they were, without exception, tenants, apparently from year to year; there is no evidence
of any lease. Even the influential Society of Lincoln's Inn does not appear
to have had any fixity of tenure... there is no trace of any lease of Lincoln's
Inn until 1472, when one John Stanney undertook to procure a lease for
90 years. It does not appear that this was ever done.

In truth (apart from the amount of the rent) nothing is known about
the terms upon which the Society held the property before 1535,
when the Bishop granted a ninety-nine years' lease to William
Sulyard. All the Registers of the Bishops before that of Bishop

---

[1] B.B. IV. 284.   [2] *Ante*, pp. 23, 41.   [3] *Ante*, p. 46.   [4] *Ante*, p. 51.
[5] B.B. IV. 283.   [6] *Ibid.* 293.

Reade who occupied the see from 1396 to 1415 are now lost[1] and
there is no reference to the Society in that Register. But while
Bishop Montague was unable to support his contention in 1635 by
any evidence which could carry weight on an adjudication of a
claim of right, there is no reason to reject it as a fiction without any
historical foundation.

There is no evidence to suggest that the Inns of that period in the
neighbourhood had been built to last for generations. Thomas de
Lincoln's Inn, which was not built before 1331, was ruinous in less
than a century. Even though the Bishop built *sumptuose*[1] he may not
have built for the future, although the description given by Matthew
Paris[2] indicates building on a scale which would be excessive for a
bishop who merely wanted an office in London and a chamber of
residence for occasional visits. If the Bishop's palace had only been
used in this way from the death of Bishop Neville in 1244 (or even
from the death of Bishop Richard in 1253) to the close of the century,
a bishop is not likely to have made much expenditure on the maintenance of a group of buildings of which he made so little use. It is
not, therefore, inherently improbable that, at any date between
1292 and 1311, they were as a whole 'very ruinous and out of repair', even if an office and a temporary place of residence there were
well maintained. Moreover, nothing would be more likely in such
circumstances than the sharing of the extensive accommodation
available between the Bishop, his officers and a community of lawyers. There is accordingly every good reason for adopting Sulyard's
version of the ancient tradition, even though it cannot be verified.
It is immune from the attack which can justly be made upon the
version propagated by Stow and his successors (including the
author of the *M.T.MS.*).

But at a time when Sulyard's version had been forgotten, and
Stow's version had been seriously discredited, the discovery of
Thomas de Lincoln's Inn came as a shock to the antiquarians, and
it was soon followed by too ready acceptance of inferences too
hastily drawn, though it still leaves difficulties unsolved. Turner,
its discoverer, was indeed still cautious. But Odgers, misled by a
misreading of the rent roll of 1399 into the belief that the Serjeant's
Inn was the only Inn on the site, and assuming (upon no evidence)
that lawyers were still in residence there at that date, evolved the
theory that they migrated to Chancery Lane between then and

[1] *Ibid.* 282.   [2] *Ante*, p. 11.

1422, taking the name with them, and Holdsworth accepted this theory as probably correct.[1] It is now clear that there were in fact two Inns upon that site—one which the Abbot had 'newly built' and the other the ruined Serjeant's Inn. The error of assuming that there was only one Inn there, as has already been pointed out,[2] vitiates the whole of the argument.

Williams, who discovered so much material relevant to those Inns, did not take the same view. His theory was that the Society was probably founded by the Serjeant, and probably migrated from his Inn to the Bishop's Inn, but that it found there on arrival a body of lawyers who might have been established there long before 1338.[3] It has already been suggested that this theory is also open to serious criticism. If it is admissible to believe (as has already been contended in this chapter) that the Bishop's Inn was occupied (even in part and even subject to reservations) by lawyers before 1338, their Society was certainly not founded by Thomas de Lincoln. If such a Society had been in occupation over such a long period of time, but was not called 'Lincoln's Inn' before 1417, it had presumably by then become known by some other name, and of this there is no trace. But there seems to be no reason why it should have abandoned the name by which it was already known because other lawyers joined it on a migration from Thomas de Lincoln's Inn, unless he was so eminent that they wanted to adopt him as their second founder. But if their purpose was to honour themselves by honouring him, his very existence could hardly have been forgotten in Lincoln's Inn some fifty years afterwards; and in fact it was.[4]

The conclusion that the reasoning of Odgers (adopted by Holdsworth) was based upon fundamental error, and that the argument of Williams is unacceptable, does not necessarily dispose of the possibility that a company of lawyers were residing in the Serjeant's Inn when he sold it in 1369, remained there and then migrated between 1399 and 1422, taking the name with them. The Abbey did not use the old Inn, or build the new Inn, for permanent occupation by monks. But there is not a jot of evidence to support what are only possibilities, and would never have been envisaged but for the duplication of the name of Lincoln's Inn and the improbability of concurrent user. This certainly has an appearance of improbability; and so has the idea that the Society had been in continuous occupation of a part of the Bishop's Inn from the time of King Edward I or

[1] *Ante*, pp. 55-57.   [2] *Ante*, p. 56.   [3] *Ante*, p. 53.   [4] *Ante*, p. 54.

II. But the early days of the Society are beset with improbabilities which tend to neutralize one another.

It is improbable that if lawyers had remained in the Serjeant's Inn after 1369, there would have been no mention anywhere of their presence. It is improbable that if the Society had been in occupation of any part of the Abbot's Inn in 1399, or in any of the ensuing years (by which time it must have reached an advanced stage of development), it would not have been mentioned in the rent roll, in either its original or its final form. If the Society had originated in Thomas de Lincoln's Inn, and had migrated from it after 1399, it is improbable that there would have been no reference to him or his Inn or the migration; and there is none, unless it be in those cryptic references to the 'farm of Lincoln's Inn'. Moreover, to postulate such a migration is not the only way, or indeed the most attractive way, of escape from the problem of concurrent use of the name, though there are difficulties along every route.

There may have been a Society of lawyers (in the Bishop's Inn or elsewhere) which had been founded by the Earl but had never actually used his name. Or again, there may have been a Society of lawyers which had no special connection with the Earl, but wanted to be named after the distinguished reformer of legal administration. Such a body would naturally be anxious to take advantage of the decay of the Serjeant's Inn to secure the use of the name; and this might have involved it in taking a tenancy of the 'farm of Lincoln's Inn', and the Abbot in changing the name of his Inn. It may truly be said that there is no evidence to support either of these possibilities. But they are no worse than the migration theory in that respect, and in other respects no less attractive. It is at this point that a consideration already mentioned comes into play. Henry de Lacy was just such a legal reformer as might be expected to found an Inn; but, on the other hand, he was just such an eminent ancestor as any Inn would wish to claim, honouring him and honoured by bearing his name, with his permission, or even perhaps without. Accordingly, it is tempting to suggest that the Society first adopted the name under unknown circumstances, at a time when Thomas de Lincoln had ceased to practise the law, under an arrangement with the Abbot, who would have no particular interest in the name. This indeed may be speculation not far wide of the mark. But on balance it appears that it ought to be resisted. The name was certainly used to describe the whole property comprising both the Abbot's Inn and the Serjeant's Inn as late as 1399, and perhaps as late as 1417. It may safely be assumed that the Society did not use the arms of the Earl before it adopted his name; and the tradition in the Inn, as related by Sulyard, was that his arms have 'been always since set up'.[1] Sulyard is first mentioned in the Black Books in 1514,[2] and some of the 'Ancients' then alive must have been born at least as early as 1450. If less than fifty years had then passed since the Society, as a deliberate act, adopted the name and arms of the Earl, it seems incredible that the transaction should have been entirely forgotten, and that the tradition that he was the founder of the Society should have by then become uniform and unquestioned. It is here that the Sulyard narrative assumes great importance, because it carries the tradition back almost to the time when the sort of event which has attracted modern speculation must have occurred, if it occurred at all. On this ground alone it is dangerous to speculate. The only speculation which is consistent with the ancient tradition necessarily involves concurrent user of the name over a long period of years. But, in spite of this, it ought perhaps to be preferred for the reasons just given. The Society would obviously be anxious to secure the *exclusive* use of the name after the Serjeant's Inn fell into decay. The Abbot's Inn had dropped the name before 1525; possibly soon after 1417. There may have been an arrangement under which the Society took a tenancy from the convent of the 'farm of Lincoln's Inn' consisting of the ruined Serjeant's Inn and the farmland, with the exclusive right to use the name, and the Abbot may thereupon have changed the name of his Inn. This is indeed mere speculation; but it is in harmony with tradition; and if mere speculation has any value at all, it is to be preferred to the speculation that there may have been a migration from the Abbot's Lincoln's Inn between 1399 and 1422.

A migration from the Serjeant's Inn, when he sold it in 1369, is an even greater improbability, because the Abbot certainly continued to use the name of Lincoln's Inn until 1399, and therefore to suggest that the lawyers carried off the name before 1399 would be to create the very problem which the migration theory has been designed to solve.

Accordingly, it seems that the theory that Thomas de Lincoln founded the Society, a theory which is not supported by any evidence, which is hedged about with improbabilities, and which does

[1] *Ante*, p. 39.   [2] B.B. I. 175.

not afford the only way, or indeed the best way, of escape from another problem, ought to be discarded.

Modern research may be said to have travelled in a full circle. Until Baildon disposed of Stow's theory that the Earl's residence was in Chancery Lane, the tradition as recorded by him was generally, though sometimes cautiously, accepted. But Baildon certainly tore a hole in it. This hole he sought to patch up by speculating upon a migration via Furnival's Inn. The contents of the *M.T.MS.* disprove this theory. Soon afterwards Thomas de Lincoln's Inn was discovered afresh, and radical theories were based upon this, which (it is suggested) may now be eliminated. Meanwhile, the rediscovery of Sulyard's earlier version of the tradition has conferred upon it additional strength and probability in three respects: (1) it is not open to the attack justifiably made upon Stow's version, and suffers from no inherent improbability; (2) it now has a longer pedigree, which indeed carries it back so far that it could hardly by that time have been uniformly accepted by the 'Ancients of the Inn', if modern theories had any validity; (3) it is not faced with competition by any alternative theory which in itself has probability.

Accordingly, the old tradition may be said to be even more firmly based than it was before Baildon began his work. But it is still an unproved tradition. There is still to be found, in some of the legal libraries and elsewhere, a mass of material bearing on the history of the Inns of Court which has never been investigated, and some remarkable chance discoveries have been made in the past century. But it is improbable that proof will ever be forthcoming of the beginnings of Lincoln's Inn, if Sulyard himself could find none. So the present position is this: if the inherited tradition must produce its birth certificate and documents of title, in truth it has none. But if the modern radicals have to prove that it is a bastard, they have signally failed in the attempt. Therefore to the question posed by Sir Frederick Pollock in his classic Address, 'Must we therefore renounce Henry de Lacy and regard our appropriation of his lion as at best a trespass excusable by lapse of time?' the writer of this Discourse would answer 'No'.

G

LIST OF AUTHORITIES,
SOURCES AND ABBREVIATIONS

Annales Londinienses, edited by Stubbs (1882)
Annales Paulini, edited by Stubbs (1882)
Archaeologia, published by the Society of Antiquaries, 2nd edn. (1779)
Athenae Oxonienses, revised edn. (1817)

Baildon, The Site of Lincoln's Inn, in B.B. IV. 263
Bailey, Introduction to 'Two *Compoti*' of the Earl's Stewards (1884)
Ball, *Lincoln's Inn* (1947)
Baxter and Johnson, *Medieval Latin Word List* (1934)
Black Books of Lincoln's Inn, 1422–1845, edited by Walker and Baildon
    (1897–1902)
Brerewood, History of the Middle Temple (1634–8). A manuscript in the
    Middle Temple Library

Camden, *Britannia* (1607)
Carr, George James Turner, 1867–1946, extracted from the *Proceedings
    of the British Academy*, vol. XL, p. 207. *The Pension Book of Clement's
    Inn* (1960)
Coke, Institutes, 4th Part (1648)
Cotton, *Discourse on the High Steward*

Dictionary of National Biography
Dugdale, *Origines Juridiciales* (1666)

Fortescue, *De Laudibus Legum Angliae* (1468–71)

Hakewill, The Liberty of the Subject against the particular Power of
    Impositions (1641)
    The manner how Statutes are enacted in Parliament (1641)
    Modus tenendi Parliamentum (1660)
Harcourt, *His Grace the Steward and Trial by Peers* (1907)
Hearne, *Curious Discourses* (1720, enlarged edn. 1771)
Holdsworth, *History of English Law*, vol. II (3rd edn. 1923). In *The Law
    Quarterly Review*, vol. XLIV (1928)
Horwood, *Yearbooks of the reign of K. Edw. I* 20/21 (1866)
Hurst, *Short History of Lincoln's Inn* (1946)

Justinian, *Institutes*

G*

Lambard, *Archeion* (1635)

Lanercost, Chronicle of, transcribed by Stevenson (1839)

Legal Antiquities, a seventeenth-century manuscript in the Middle Temple Library

Lexicon manuale ad Scriptores mediae et infimae Latinitatis (1866)

Middle Temple manuscript on Lincoln's Inn (1620–28)

Odgers, Essay no. 12 in *Essays in Legal History*, edited by Vinogradoff (1913)

Parliament Roll

Patent Roll

Pollock, *The Origins of the Inns of Court*. In *The Law Quarterly Review*, vol. XLVIII (1932)

Prince, *Worthies of Devon* (1701)

Prynne, *Aurum Reginae* (1668)

Rolls of Parliament

Russell, *The Lord High Steward of England* (1776)

Rymer, *Foedera*

Stow, *Survey of London* (1598)

Stubbs, *Annales Londinienses* and *Annales Paulini* in one volume (1882)
Constitutional History (1906)

Sulyard (d. 1540). Extracts from a lost manuscript quoted in the Middle Temple manuscript on Lincoln's Inn

Tate, *Discourse on the High Steward* (1603)

Thorne, Lecture in Gray's Inn, published in *Graya*, no. 50 (1959)

Thynne, *Discourse on the Antiquity of the Houses of Law*.

Townsend, *Discourse on the High Steward* (1603)

Turner, Lincoln's Inn, a Pamphlet (1903). In the *Athenaeum*, 22 September 1906

Weever, *Ancient Funerall Monuments* (1631)

Williams, *Early Holborn* (1927); *Staple Inn* (1906)

ABBREVIATIONS

B.B.	Black Books of Lincoln's Inn, edited by Walker and Baildon
M.T.MS.	The Middle Temple Manuscript on Lincoln's Inn
W.D.	The documents printed in Williams, *Early Holborn*

INDEX